J.-J. SERVAN-SCHREIBER

The American Challenge

TRANSLATED FROM THE FRENCH BY
RONALD STEEL

WITH A FOREWORD BY
ARTHUR SCHLESINGER, Jr.

HAMISH HAMILTON
LONDON

First published in Great Britain, 1968
by Hamish Hamilton Ltd
90 Great Russell Street, London WCI
Copyright © 1967 by Editions Denoel as Le Défi Américain
English Translation copyright © 1968 by Atheneum House, Inc.
Foreword copyright © by Arthur Schlesinger, Jr.

SBN 241 01582 0

Printed in Great Britain by
Western Printing Services Ltd Bristol

If you give a man a fish,
he will have a single meal.
If you teach him how to fish,
he will eat all his life.

Kuan-tzu

Note

In this translation the word 'billion' is used in its French and American sense of one thousand million.

Contents

PART 4

Counterattack

PART 5

The Political Question

PART 6

The Wellsprings of Power

FOREWORD *Arthur Schlesinger, Jr.*

The American Challenge is a book about the crisis of Europe. It has already had an extraordinary impact. In France no book since the war, fiction or non-fiction, sold so many copies in its first three months. Throughout Europe politicians and civil servants, editors and professors, bankers, industrialists and engineers are studying and quoting it. It has had this impact because M. Servan-Schreiber has stated the dilemma of Europe with brilliant clarity, precision and urgency, and because he has had the further audacity to point the way to a solution. If Europeans respond to his appeal by acting on this book as well as by reading it, *The American Challenge* may do for European unity very much what Thomas Paine's *Common Sense* did for American independence.

Europe, M. Servan-Schreiber says, is in decline. No one, he warns, should be deceived by the existence of the European Economic Community. Either the EEC had to become more than a Common Market, or else it would revert to national patterns. Since it has not moved towards integration, it is beginning to move towards disintegration. Only the Americans, moreover, have understood and seized the opportunities created by the Common Market. The result has been the economic invasion of Europe by the United States. If present tendencies continue, the third industrial power in the world, after America and Russia, could be, not Europe, but American industry in Europe. The present European generation has only a few years to decide between restoring an autonomous European civilization or allowing Europe to become a subsidiary of the United States.

In evoking the American spectre, M. Servan-Schreiber may

sound for a moment like General de Gaulle. But he differs
sharply from the General both in diagnosis and in remedy.
General de Gaulle sees the United States as bent on the establishment of world hegemony. He attributes the economic
invasion, as he said in his press conference of 27 November
1967, 'not so much to the organic superiority of the United
States as to the dollar inflation that it is exporting to others
under the cover of the gold exchange standard'. He advocates
defensive measures to seal off Europe from American economic
penetration and political influence. M. Servan-Schreiber's
analysis is both subtler and more profound. He sees the American challenge as the result of the dynamism of American
society. And he advocates not the insulation of Europe from
America but its salvation through discriminating Americanization.

Wherein does the secret of American dynamism lie? Not the
least fascinating aspect of this book for American readers is the
portrait they will find of their own country. The secret does not
lie, as de Gaulle (and Lenin) would insist, in the pressure of
surplus American capital for investment outlets abroad;
M. Servan-Schreiber argues that nine-tenths of American investment in Europe is financed out of European resources. Nor does
it lie in American plans for political dominion; M. Servan-
Schreiber rejects conspiratorial explanations. Nor does it lie in
American scientific and technological superiority; he has no
difficulty in showing how many basic discoveries were first made
in European laboratories.

The disparity lies rather, M. Servan-Schreiber contends, in
the 'art of organization'—in the mobilization of intelligence and
talent to conquer not only invention but development, production and marketing. He thus defines the 'gap', to use the hope-
less current jargon, as less technological than managerial.
American industry spills out across the world primarily because
of the energy released by the American system—by the opportunity for individual initiative, by the innovative knack of
teams, by the flexibility of business structure and by the decentralization of business decision.

Yes, some Americans will no doubt comfortably reflect at
this point; the Frenchman is right; free enterprise is best. But
this is not at all what M. Servan-Schreiber means. He sees in the

United States not the unfettered workings of competitive capitalism but something very different: a highly organized economic system, based on enormously large units, nourished by an industrial-academic-governmental complex and stimulated, financed and guided by the national government. And he does not stop there. To speak of a 'managerial gap' is really too superficial; the real gap is institutional and cultural. In the end M. Servan-Schreiber traces American dynamism to the social mobility, the individual responsibility, the equalitarian thrust of American life and, above all, to the determination to invest in human beings, especially through the promotion of education. 'All clichés to the contrary, American society wagers much more on human intelligence than it wastes on gadgets.' The real American secret, he concludes, is the discovery that social justice, far from being the enemy of economic growth, is the necessary technical conditions for growth in an industrial society. He charitably refrains from suggesting that the United States has not yet pursued this lesson to the end, particularly in the domain of race.

From this perspective, the European problem is not so much economic or scientific as it is cultural and political. Beginning with General de Gaulle's premise about the overshadowing might of the United States, M. Servan-Schreiber reaches the opposite conclusion. The hope for Europe, he believes, lies in genuine democratization and genuine unification on all levels; it lies in the reform of education, the rejection of inherited social and intellectual rigidities, the modernization of organization and the extension of planning. If Europe really wishes to escape American domination, there is only the way of federalism and social justice. All this, in M. Servan-Schreiber's view, implies Great Britain as a part of Europe; for British scientific and technological skill are necessary if Europe is to have any weight in the world of electronic computers, automated information systems, space technology and atomic energy. British entry into the Common Market, in short, is essential to realize de Gaulle's dream of European independence. And a strong and progressive Europe, he rightly contends (only barely mentioning Vietnam), is vital to save the United States from the temptations and illusions of superpowership: Europe holds in her hands more than her own destiny.

The American Challenge is a manifesto to the European generation of which Jean-Jacques Servan-Schreiber himself is a remarkable representative. Born in 1924, he escaped from France in 1943, received training as a pilot in the United States and joined the Free French Air Force. After the war he wrote on foreign policy for *Le Monde* and then established his own weekly magazine of opinion, *L'Express*. The Algerian War was now the preoccupying issue; and Servan-Schreiber's lucid and caustic editorials helped mobilize sentiment against the French government. Perhaps in retaliation, the French government soon mobilized him and sent him to Algeria. After serving his tour of duty, he wrote a book *Lieutenant in Algeria,* which led to his indictment on the ground of supposed injury to the morale of the French Army; in due course, he was acquitted. In the last years of the war he lived under constant threat of assassination from the enthusiasts of the OAS.

When France finally pulled out of Algeria, Servan-Schreiber converted *L'Express* into a highly successful news weekly, rather as if the *New Republic* were to make itself over on the model of *Time*. In addition to these and other publishing ventures, he has been active in politics, working closely in the fifties with Pierre Mendès-France and in the sixties with Gaston Defferre. His wit and objectivity of expression, his commitment to reasoned argument, his political activism and his personal valour—all stamp him as a European of the Kennedy generation and style. It would not be surprising if he himself were to take a prominent role in shaping the European response to the American challenge.

ARTHUR SCHLESINGER, JR.

INTRODUCTION

THIS book develops an inquiry that began with a factual observation but has far-reaching implications.

Starting with a rather matter-of-fact examination of American investment in Europe, we find an economic system which is in a state of collapse. It is our own. We see a foreign challenger breaking down the political and psychological framework of our societies. We are witnessing the prelude to our own historical bankruptcy.

At times like this we naturally think about reinforcing the barricades to hold back the invader. But purely defensive measures might well make us even weaker. In trying to understand why this is so, we stumble across the key element. This war—and it is a war—is being fought not with dollars, or oil, or steel, or even with modern machines. It is being fought with creative imagination and organizational talent.

At least a dozen European authorities have known this, and have been trying to tell us for some time. But no one has been paying any attention. This inquiry is based on what these men have seen, explained, and analysed.

Those whose job it is to lead us and keep us informed have been casually looking at each individual piece of the puzzle. Now it is time to concentrate on the problem as a whole. This strange phenomenon, so dangerous, so massive in its size and power, is hypnotizing and overwhelming. From our present ignorance we could sink into total despair.

The day may indeed come when we can only sit by helplessly and watch Europe disappear as a centre of civilization. But that day is not yet here, and there is still time to act.

xiii

Act how? Fight against what? We have less to fear from the absence of a European will than from its lack of direction.

General Motors, after all, isn't the Wehrmacht. The fight for the ownership of Machines Bull isn't Munich. And the supersonic Concorde jet isn't the battle of Sedan. This is the first full-scale war to be fought without arms or armour. If we had another André Malraux today, he would tug our heartstrings not with tales of the heroism of the fighters at Terruel, but with the fabulous struggle for the conquest of Titan's metal, or the ferocious effort to master the mental world of integrated circuits.

Even without a great lyric poet to recount them, the facts themselves are charged with power and emotion. It is enough to watch American investment skim gently across the earth like the fabled swallow, and watch what it takes away, how 'it thrusts, twists, enfolds, tears away, carries off, breaks open, and attacks'. Here is how it is done.

PART I

THE ASSAULT ON EUROPE

THE ART OF EUROPE

CHAPTER I

THE SWEETEST DEAL

FIFTEEN years from now it is quite possible that the world's third greatest industrial power, just after the United States and Russia, will not be Europe, but *American industry in Europe*. Already, in the ninth year of the Common Market, this European market is basically American in organization.

The importance of U.S. penetration rests, first of all, on the sheer amount of capital invested—currently about $14 billion ($14,000,000,000).[1] Add to this the massive size of the firms carrying out this conquest. Recent efforts by European firms to centralize and merge are due largely to the need to compete with the American giants like International Business Machines (IBM) and General Motors. This is direct penetration. But there is another aspect of the problem which is considerably more subtle.[2]

Every day an American banker working in Paris gets requests from French firms looking for Frenchmen 'with experience in an American corporation'. The manager of a German steel mill hires only staff personnel 'having been trained with an American firm'. The British Marketing Council sends fifty British executives to spend a year at the Harvard Business School—and the British government foots the bill. For European firms, conservative and jealous of their independence, there is now one common denominator: American methods.

[1] In *fixed assets*—that is, plant and equipment, not including working capital (about as much again). Source: U.S. Department of Commerce.

[2] This chapter is based on a special report issued by the European offices of McGraw-Hill, Inc., the leading American firm dealing in economic information.

3

During the past ten years Americans in Europe have made more mistakes than their competitors—but they have tried to correct them. And an American firm can change its methods in almost no time compared to a European firm. The Americans have been reorganizing their European operations. Everywhere they are setting up European-scale headquarters responsible for the firm's Continental business, with sweeping powers of decision, and instructions not to pay any attention to national boundaries.

These U.S. subsidiaries have shown a flexibility and adaptability that have enabled them to adjust to local conditions and be prepared for political decisions taken, or even contemplated, by the Common Market.

Since 1958 American corporations have invested $10 billion in Western Europe—*more than a third* of their total investment abroad. Of the 6,000 new businesses started overseas by Americans during that period, *half* were in Europe.[3]

One by one, American firms are setting up headquarters to coordinate their activities throughout Western Europe. This is true federalism—the only kind that exists in Europe on an industrial level. And it goes a good deal further than anything Common Market experts ever imagined.

Union Carbide set up its European headquarters in Lausanne in 1965. The Corn Products Company, which now has ten European branches, moved its coordinating office from Zurich to Brussels and transformed it into a central headquarters. IBM now directs all its European activities from Paris. The Celanese Corporation of America has recently set up headquarters in Brussels; and American Express has established its European offices in London.

Standard Oil of New Jersey has put its European oil (Esso

[3] Measures announced by President Johnson in January 1968 will partially reduce the U.S. payments deficit by reducing the amount of dollars going overseas. But, as we shall see in the next chapter, the growing economic dominance of American industry is no longer merely 'a matter of money'. Nor is the eventual decline of direct investment in Europe in itself a factor in the balance. Indeed, it is quite the contrary (see page 18)—which is why European governments were so alarmed when these economic measures were announced.

Europe) headquarters in London, and its European chemical (Esso Chemical SA) command in Brussels. Both have been told to 'ignore the present division between the Common Market and the free trade zone [Britain, Scandinavia]'. For Esso, Europe now represents a market *larger than the United States*, and one growing *three times faster*.

Monsanto has moved its international department from St. Louis to Brussels, where Mr. Throdahl, one of its vice-presidents, directs not only European operations, but all business outside the United States. Monsanto is now building factories in France, Italy, Luxembourg, Britain, and Spain, and preparing plants for Scotland and Ireland. Half of its sales now come from Europe.

The greater wealth of American corporations allows them to conduct business in Europe faster and more flexibly than their European competitors. This *flexibility* of the Americans, even more than their wealth, is their major weapon. While Common Market officials are still looking for a law which will permit the creation of European-wide businesses, American firms, with their own headquarters, already form the framework of a real 'Europeanization'.

A leading Belgian banker recently stated: 'The Common Market won't be able to work out a European corporate law in time, and during the next few years U.S. corporations will enjoy a decisive advantage over their European rivals.' The American giants in Europe become bigger and stronger all the time, and are hiring 'development' experts whose job is to seek new acquisitions.

While all this has been going on, the Europeans have done little to take advantage of the new market. On the industrial level Europe has almost nothing to compare with the dynamic American corporations being set up on her soil. The one interesting exception is Imperial Chemical Industries (Britain), the only European firm to establish a continental-scale headquarters to administer its fifty subsidiaries.

Efforts of other European corporations are timid by comparison. Among these the best known is the film company Agfa (part of the Bayer group), which two years ago decided to merge with its Belgian rival, Gevaert. But it was not a very romantic marriage. The two companies exchanged directors, put a hyphen between their names (Agfa-Gevaert), and combined their research departments. That's about all. Aside from that, they have announced their intention to form a truly unified firm the day the Common Market gives the go-ahead by passing a still non-existent statute permitting European-wide corporations. They are still waiting for legislation.

In the meantime, American firms continue to carve up Europe at their pleasure. In the words of a report by McGraw-Hill: 'The creators of the Common Market, men like Robert Schuman, Jean Monnet, and Walter Hallstein, can be proud of helping break down the barriers dividing Europe. But it is American business that has understood their idea and is helping Europe discover itself by applying, with a few variations, the same methods America used to build its own enormous market.'

Europeans especially envy the ease with which American firms reorganize themselves to tap the full potential of the new market, and they are very much aware of the advantages this flexibility offers. The question they ask me most often, says an American executive working in France, is simply: 'How do you do it?'

Hand in hand with this industrial penetration is another giant U.S. business taking shape in Europe—the creation of management consultant organizations.

The three American consultant firms with European branches (Booz, Allen and Hamilton, Arthur D. Little, Inc., and McKinsey and Co.) have *doubled* their staff *every year* for the past five years. The Americans are building a 'market consciousness' around themselves.

According to an American executive in Frankfurt: 'If a German manager wants to increase his production, he studies all the factors that go into the manufacture of his product. But if I want to increase my production, I add to these same calculations our research and market predictions so that I will know not only *how* to produce, but how to produce the desired quantity at the lowest cost. What interests me is my profit margin. What interests my European competitor is a factory that produces. *It isn't the same thing.*' This science of marketing is new in Europe. Nonetheless, there is hardly a major European executive today who does not put it at the top of his list of his concerns.

Thus, even beyond massive U.S. investments, it is American-style management that is, in its own special way, unifying Europe. As the American businessman from Frankfurt, quoted earlier, added: 'The Treaty of Rome is the sweetest deal ever to come out of Europe. It's what brought us here. We're happy to be here. We're making money. And we're going to make a lot more. Whether the political negotiations in Brussels move ahead or not, prospects in commerce and industry are better for us here than they are in the United States.'

It really is the sweetest deal anyone ever thought of. But why for them and not for us? Why do they succeed better over here than we do ourselves? In the search for the answer to this question, a whole new world opens up.

CHAPTER 2

NOT A QUESTION OF MONEY

MOST people in Western Europe think that the problem of American investment is obscure and technical, something that ought to be left to financiers and economists. It almost never comes up in political debates, and its implications are lost on those concerned with public affairs, and even on members of the government. Outside of a few experts, almost no one understands it. Terms like 'technological gap' and 'managerial gap' have become tired clichés even before we understand what they mean.

The problem is a subtle one for many reasons. It is not that we are being inundated by an excess of U.S. dollars which the Americans cannot use and which flow to the Common Market because of a temporary set of circumstances. On the contrary, it is something quite new and considerably more serious—the extension to Europe of an art of *organization* that is still a mystery to us.

The Common Market has become a new Far West for American businessmen. Their investments do not so much involve a transfer of capital, as an actual *seizure of power* within the European economy. Statistics fail to reflect the real gravity of the problem. This is why a group of economists from the six Common Market nations recently spent a year working on a more detailed analysis.[1]

American industrial investment, represented by U.S. firms in

[1] The document from which we have taken much of the information in this chapter will be published in 1968 by Walter Bruclain under the title *American Big Business and the Future of the Common Market*.

8

Europe, is currently less than 10 per cent of the total capitalization of all corporations (except in Belgium). This figure, however, has to be modified by analysing the current *growth rate* of these investments.

The U.S. Department of Commerce finds it 'striking' that from 1965 to 1966 American investment rose by 17 per cent in the United States, 21 per cent in the rest of the world, and *40 per cent in the Common Market*. These figures dramatize how the Common Market has become the New Frontier of American industry, its promised land.

A survey of leading American industrialists by the investment banking firm Donaldson, Lufkin and Jenrette, reveals that in the future these firms will consider it normal to invest 20 to 30 per cent of their assets in Europe. Although such levels have not yet been reached, this survey confirms the likelihood of an even higher growth rate for American investments in the years ahead.

Even more important than the growth rate are the *qualitative* aspects of American investment.

There is a crucial disproportion between investments made by Europeans in the United States, which are usually little more than the purchase of securities, and investments made by Americans in Europe, which often involve a real seizure of control.

It is a historical rule that a country politically and economically strong makes direct investments (and thus gains control) in less-developed countries. Thus European capital used to flow into Africa — not for simple investment, but to gain economic power and exploit local resources. Economically weak countries, suffering from the reverse side of the same classic law, see their savings seep away to the stronger countries in the form of investments. This is precisely what is happening today in the underdeveloped countries of Africa, where the property-owning classes invest their savings in Europe.

Most striking of all is the *strategic* character of American industrial penetration. One by one, U.S. corporations capture those sectors of the economy most technologically advanced, most adaptable to change, and with the highest growth rates.

As early as 1963 Gilles Bertin showed that American firms in France controlled 40 per cent of the petroleum market, 65 per cent of the production of films and photographic paper, 65 per cent of farm machinery, 65 per cent of telecommunications equipment, and 45 per cent of synthetic rubber, among others.[2] The most important sector of the economy, however, and the one most crucial for the future, is electronics. Here it is easy to see the direct link between the role of American firms and a high degree of technology involved in production. American corporations in Europe control:

15 per cent of the production of consumer goods—radio and TV, recording devices, etc.;

50 per cent of semi-conductors—replacements for old electronic tubes;

80 per cent of computers—electronic calculating machines which, among other things, transform the management of corporations;

95 per cent of the new market for integrated circuits—miniature units crucial to guided missiles and the new generation of computers.

These figures are important to keep in mind, for electronics is not an ordinary industry: it is the base upon which the next stage of industrial development depends. In the nineteenth century the first industrial revolution replaced manual labour by machines. We are now living in the *second industrial revolution*, and every year we are replacing the labour of human brains by a new kind of machine—computers.

A country which has to buy most of its electronic equipment abroad will be in a condition of inferiority similar to that of nations in the last century which were incapable of industrializing. Despite their brilliant past, these nations remained outside the mainstream of civilization. If Europe continues to lag behind in electronics, she could cease to be included among the advanced areas of civilization within a single generation.[3]

The least-known aspect of American investment in Europe is how it is financed. Financing investments is less and less a problem for American corporations. With their scope, capabilities and techniques, they have no trouble finding money on the local market to pay for their factories.

[2] From *Foreign Investment in France* by Gilles Bertin, graduate of the University of California and professor of economics.

[3] According to forecasts made by the Hudson Institute on the world thirty years from now. *See* next chapter.

During 1965 the Americans invested $4 billion in Europe.[4] This is where the money came from:

1. Loans from the European capital market (Euro-issues) and direct credits from European countries—55 per cent.
2. Subsidies from European governments and internal financing from local earnings—35 per cent.
3. Direct dollar transfers from the United States—10 per cent.

Thus, nine-tenths of American investment in Europe is financed from European sources. In other words, *we pay them to buy us.*

In 1966 the Euro-dollar market supplied American corporations with $450 to $500 million. This is private capital directly connected to the U.S. payments deficit.[5] These Euro-dollars, earned by Europeans from sales to the United States, form a protected financial market and are loaned to subsidiaries of American firms. European corporations, by contrast, rarely have the means to join this exclusive financial club.

The remainder of financing for U.S. investments is assured, as we have seen, first by the resources of American-owned subsidiaries in Europe (internal financing), whose profits generally exceed that of European firms by 50 per cent, and secondly by subsidies from European governments.

Thus, while the European nations are in principle trying to form an economic community, they have in fact opened the gate to increasingly intense competition by granting direct government subsidies to attract American investments.

In order not to violate the provisions of the Treaty of Rome, they provide a pretext for these subsidies by saying they are necessary to help regional development. As competition within the Common Market has raised new regional problems

[4] Figures taken from the *Survey of Current Business.*

[5] Since 1960 between $1 and $3 billion have left the United States every year. Part of this goes into central banks—which is a familiar monetary problem. But another part stays in the hands of commercial or industrial banks. A European firm that sells its products to the United States and receives dollars in payment is not obliged to deposit them in its own bank. The French have had this freedom only since 1967, but it has existed for some time in most other European countries. Thus some very important free dollar accounts have been created in Europe. These are called Euro-dollars.

(particularly in areas dependent on traditional industries such as coal and steel), and as a general slowdown of economic growth has created unemployment problems, European nations have been pouring funds into regional assistance without ever working out a common programme among themselves. The major beneficiaries have been American investors.

The Belgian government, for example, passed a law in 1966 allowing subsidies in the form of capital grants up to 30 per cent of the value of foreign investment. The Dutch went a step further by raising this subsidy to 40 per cent. Foreign investors also benefit from other hidden benefits, ranging from bargain prices for industrial sites, to advantageous tax laws and special rates for gas and electricity.

When an American corporation decides to cross the Atlantic and set up shop in Europe, it doesn't much care where it locates its plant. It can, so to speak, put itself up for auction among the competing European governments to make the best deal. And it gets what it wants.

The final handicap European business suffers in competition with its American rivals, and probably the most serious one of all, is the systematic and organized assistance the U.S. government gives to key industries through its contracts and research grants.

A good example of this is the American electronics industry, which does *63 per cent of its business* in the form of government contracts, compared to 12 per cent for European industry. In the critical field of research and development, the government foots 85 per cent of the bill, compared to 50 per cent in the Common Market. Calculated as a percentage of sales, European research funds are less than half those in the United States.

These figures show the overwhelming superiority now enjoyed by key American industries. This superiority is both current and potential: it is based on present capacity to invest and on the strength of the growth rate.

The invasion of American industrial power has only just begun, and its growing impact poses a grave problem for every government in Europe. In the words of M. Boyer de la Giroday of the Brussels commission, 'American investment in Europe has its own special nature. When we set up the European Economic Community (EEC) we did something useful, but simple and still incomplete. So far its major result has been to speed our economic prosperity by creating the most favourable climate for a *growing invasion of American industries*. They are the only ones that have acted on the logic of the Common Market.'

What can we do about it? According to De la Giroday: 'Any attempt to discourage or restrict U.S. investment in Europe would only work to our disadvantage, both economically and technologically, without bringing us anything in return. What's more, such an attempt would threaten the very existence of the Common Market—which no one has any intention of doing. Even the French government, after having thought that it could curb American investment on its soil, has had to let it expand.'

Governments and businessmen have been troubled by the problem for some time because it is so enormous and the answers so complicated. Restricting or prohibiting investments is no answer, since this would only slow down our own development. Yet if Europe continues to sit by passively as U.S. investments flood the Continent, our whole economic system will be controlled by the Americans.

Hans Dichgans, a member of the German parliament, said in March 1965: 'History teaches us that in the long run a healthy economy must free itself from dependence on foreign capital and rely on its own resources. The United States itself furnishes the best example of this.'

But the economic system must be strong enough to do it. The weak and underdeveloped countries take extreme attitudes towards foreign investment. Either they supinely tolerate their own exploitation or they react violently by prohibiting such investment entirely and by nationalizing foreign firms. A modern society like Europe can hardly afford to take such an attitude. In so far as foreign investment merely reflects a superior technology, we could only nationalize the factory walls. You can't expropriate technical know-how and inventive skills.

The European nations have made scattered attempts to deal with this problem, which have been summarized in Reiner Hellmann's book, *Amerika auf dem Europa Markt*.[6] Let's see what he says.

[6] *America in the Common Market* by Reiner Hellmann (Baden-Baden).

The French government has changed its policies three times. From 1959 to 1963 it encouraged foreign investment. On 1 July 1959, the premier, Michel Debré, wrote: 'If U.S. firms are going to set up plants in the Common Market, it is better, under any circumstances, that they choose France rather than her partners.' No argument here.

Later public opinion began to focus on the social problems, some of them rather startling, caused by American take-overs. Remington Rand at Caluire. Chrysler bought out Simca and Libby set up plants in Bas-Rhone/Languedoc. Finally there was the unfortunate sale of the Machines Bull computer firm to General Electric. In response to these incidents the new French government under premier Georges Pompidou launched a restrictive policy. Its most immediate and direct effect was the transfer of American investment funds to other Common Market countries.

The plant General Motors was supposed to have put up in Strasbourg was switched to Germany.[7] Ford had picked Thionville as a site, and instead went to Belgium. Phillips Petroleum planned on Bordeaux, and gave it up for the Benelux countries. In our already tough competition with our partners, we handed them another weapon: the technological and marketing skills that go hand in hand with American investment.

Then in early 1966 a third French government, this one under both Pompidou and Debré, reversed this policy—with its temporary psychological advantages and its grave economic drawbacks—and allowed American investments to re-enter France on an ostensibly selective basis.

A Common Market country that takes a more restrictive attitude than its partners toward American investment only helps its competitors at its own expense.

The British Labour government, for example, faithful to its philosophy of greater government control over the economy, was initially far more critical towards American investments than the Conservatives. Prime Minister Harold Wilson has been an ardent advocate of the need for Europeans to form a great technological power capable of competing with the United States. On numerous occasions he has declared that the primary

[7] Later the French government changed its policy, so it is back in Strasbourg again.

objective of Europe must be 'to prevent the domination of our economy by the Americans'.

But since Britain, like the others, is isolated in her reactions and faces the danger of being outbid by her trade rivals, this theory is not so easy to put into practice. In 1964, when Labour was in the opposition, Chrysler acquired a substantial minority interest in the big motor firm, Rootes. The Labour party protested vehemently. But in 1967, when the Labourites were in power, Chrysler announced it was taking full control of Rootes. After studying the problem, the Wilson government rejected trade-union demands for nationalizing Rootes, and then gave the green light to Chrysler.

In Germany there has been an equally subtle, but quite opposite, development since the change of chancellor. After a long period of free-wheeling economic liberalism inspired by political motives, German industrialists began to show alarm. As early as 1965 the Commertzbank estimated American-controlled investments in Germany at $2 billion, while the gross capital of all firms quoted on the German stock exchange was only $3·5 billion. It was clearly time to act. When Mobil Oil tried to take over the German firm Aral in 1967, the government demanded that control be limited to 28 per cent and that stockholders pass a resolution affirming 'they agree that the German identity of the firm shall be maintained'.

While it was that the British government discovered it could not rigidly apply its own doctrine of control, and the German government that it could not stick to the tenets of economic liberalism, the French government wobbled from one position to the other. Italy and the Benelux countries, which in 1963 rejected the French request for joint controls over U.S. investments in the Common Market, now have begun to worry about the problem. They affirm their intention to 'restrict American investments to the general objectives of the national development plan'. The formula is too vague to be much of a restraint, and too theoretical to be applied. The problem always boils down to the same thing: purely national efforts at control simply induce the Americans to transfer their investments to another country. This is hardly an answer.

The most instructive response has recently come from European businessmen and executives who are members of an organization known as UNICE (Union National des Industries de la Communauté Européenne, or in English, the European Community Industrial Union). This year they passed a declaration of principle that deserves wider attention.

It begins with a reference to the classic principles of economic liberalism, or what is known in the United States simply as the free-market economy: 'Industry is fundamentally devoted to the principle of the free flow of capital and the freedom to establish new businesses. Thus it takes a positive and liberal attitude towards American investments and the establishment of American firms in the Common Market.

'In this spirit we affirm that if measures are taken to provide more information on the movement of capital from other countries, these measures must under no circumstance constitute an obstacle to the entry of foreign capital into the Common Market, nor affect the way it is disbursed.'

After this declaration of principle, which deals with the problem in a logic that seems reasonable, the management group then carefully raises a few of its 'concerns':

'American investments should not be allowed to reach such a level that the economies of European countries, or key economic areas, become too dependent on decisions based primarily on the needs of American economic policy, or on those of the management of American corporations.'

An excellent declaration, as explicit and as justified as the first—except that it means the exact opposite.

After dealing with these two themes, the UNICE manifesto goes on to more serious matters—such as the real fears of these businessmen:

1. 'American investment posed no problem so long as American industry did not rely on the European capital market, which it is now doing heavily. There is a serious danger that the demands now made by American business on the European capital market are at the expense of European firms seeking capital funds.' This is conflict number one.

2. The second one is even more important. 'While in certain areas the establishment of American plants has helped create new jobs (in Italy, for example), in most of the other countries where there is pressure on the labour market, the search for workers by American firms has caused problems. These prob-

lems are intensified by the methods used by the Americans in recruiting personnel and by the conditions they offer.' If the first criticism is that the Americans dry up the capital market, the second is that they force salary hikes because they offer higher wages.

3. Third criticism: American firms knock down prices. Without even bothering to disguise its motives, UNICE criticizes foreign rivals for failing to respect the cartels and arrangements designed to maintain profit margins. 'It has become clear', states the manifesto, 'that certain American firms have been badly informed about the price mechanisms used in the European market—mechanisms which the various Continental rivals respect. A joint study of production costs has allowed us to set up rules which, while safeguarding competition, prove beneficial to all. We must not allow the American firms, from lack of knowledge of our methods, to provoke a price war that would cause serious difficulties in the market.'

Stimulation of the financial market, better wages, better prices: few arguments could be as persuasive as these in convincing anyone of the wisdom of liberal economic policy towards American investments. Foreign investment, in other words, is shaking the habits and attitudes of political leaders and businessmen. They haven't yet worked out any clear policy, but some have woken up and a few have become seriously alarmed.

The scope for action is limited. Any restrictive national policy would raise more serious problems than the American investments themselves. The only level on which policy can be made, and put into action, is that of the Community itself—provided that we go to the heart of the problem. To avoid useless polemics, we must admit once and for all that American investment brings important, and even irreplaceable, benefits.[8]

Above all we must not forget that this investment is not a cause, but an *effect*. It is the result of a series of faults which together explain why European industry lags behind American

---

[8] The best study to date on the *fertilization* of the Common Market by foreign investment is *Transatlantic Investments*, by Christopher Layton. He notes that 'without the vigorous competition induced by American investment, European businessmen would not be talking about the need for concentration and merger as they do today'.

industry. If we deprive ourselves of the injection of dynamism, organization, innovation, and boldness that characterize the giant American corporations, we will fall even further behind. Before deciding how to counterattack, we should first examine the technological benefits that accompany American investment.

It is the giant American firms, not medium-sized ones, that play the major role in penetrating the European market. More than half of U.S. subsidiaries in Europe belong to the 340 American firms appearing on the list of the 500 largest corporations in the world. Three American giants are responsible for 40 per cent of direct American investment in France, Germany, and Britain. We know that 85 per cent of industrial research and development funds in the United States are conducted by corporations that employ more than 5,000 people. Because of their vast resources, these are the firms that can help us close the 'technology gap' between Europe and America.[9]

Also, it is worth noting that any deliberately restrictive policy towards American investment in Europe would automatically substitute two further dangers.

First, a flow of manufactured products would replace the flow of capital, and particularly easily since most tariff barriers were lowered by the Kennedy Round. After having raised walls against American capital, should we then build new ones against American products? This would merely assure our own underdevelopment. For most items of advanced technology, whose price is high because of the need to amortize research expenses, American products are virtually irreplaceable under current conditions. You cannot control the international computer market by juggling tariffs.

In an unpublished monograph, Donald B. Keesing, a young economist at Columbia University, has itemized the American share of Western trade in industries of advanced technology.

[9] A study by the Chase Manhattan Bank shows the relation between research expenses and the number of investment operations in the Community by American firms: during the past eight years nearly 70 per cent of such operations have been made in the three fields of electrical engineering, mechanical engineering, and the chemical industry. Together they comprise 80 per cent of research expenditure.

He shows that the greater the degree of technological advancement (measured by the number of scientists and engineers as percentage of total number of employees), the greater the American role. Thus, by suppressing American *investment* in Europe, we would only intensify the need to import *products* made in the United States.

The second danger, after replacing capital for products, would be substituting the *investments themselves.* American firms irritated with restrictions imposed by the Common Market would simply move, as they have often done already, to Britain, Scandinavia, Spain, and their free-trade-zone associates. This would allow them to benefit automatically from the tariff reductions worked out between these countries and the Common Market.

In short, Europeans are faced with a dilemma, that, without exaggeration, is of historic importance.

If we allow American investments to enter freely under present conditions, we consign European industry—or at least the part that is most scientifically and technologically advanced and on which our future rests—to a subsidiary role, and Europe herself to the position of a satellite.

If, on the other hand, we adopt effective restrictive measures, we would be double losers—denying ourselves both the manufactured products we need and the capital funds that would then be invested in other countries. By trying to be self-sufficient we would only condemn ourselves to underdevelopment.

What can we do? The problem of American investments is not an isolated case. It is only one special aspect of the problem of power, of the growing displacement of power between Europe and America.

Nothing would be more absurd than to treat the American investor as 'guilty', and to respond by some form of repression. No matter how determined we are that Europe be mistress of her destiny, we ought not to forget what Alexander Hamilton said in 1791 about foreign investment in the United States: 'Rather than treating the foreign investor as a rival, we should consider him a valuable helper, for he increases our production and the efficiency of our businesses.'

If American investment is really part of the phenomenon of power, the problem for Europe is to become a great power.

What today seems like an enormous 'rummage sale' of our industry to the Americans could, paradoxically, lead to our salvation. 'Nothing is spurring Europe more strongly toward the means of her own rescue than the U.S. economic challenge.'[10] American power is no longer what it was after the end of the war. Its scale and even its nature have changed. We are learning about it because we are feeling its impact right here on our shores. This is all to the good. While it is a shock, shock is better than surprise because it forces us to pay attention.

During the *past ten years*, from the end of the cold war and the launching of the first Sputnik, American power has made an unprecedented leap forward. It has undergone a violent and productive internal revolution. Technological innovation has now become the basic objective of economic policy. In America today the government official, the industrial manager, the economics professor, the engineer, and the scientist have joined forces to develop coordinated techniques for integrating factors of production. These techniques have stimulated what amounts to a permanent industrial revolution. The Americans call it 'cross-fertilization'.

The originality of this revolution consists precisely in the effect this fusion of talents has on decisions made by government agencies, corporations, and universities. This takes us a long way from the old image of the United States—a country where business was not only separate from government but constantly struggling with it, and where there was a chasm between intellectuals and businessmen. Today, on the contrary, this combination of forces has produced the remarkable integrated entity that John Kenneth Galbraith calls a 'techno-structure'.

If we continue to allow the major decisions on industrial innovation, on technological creativity—decisions which directly affect our lives—to be made in Washington, New York, Cambridge, Detroit, Seattle, and Houston, there is a real danger that Europe may for ever be confined to second place. We may not be able to build one of those great industrial-intellectual complexes on which a technologically creative society depends. The power, the speed, the pervasive nature of American invest-

[10] *Newsweek* 27 February 1967, p. 38.

ment are a warning and a challenge to us. What kind of future
do we want?

It is time for us to take stock and face the hard truth. Some
of those who watched the decline of Rome or Byzantium also
caught a glimpse of the future that was coming. But that was not
enough to change the course of history. If we are to be master
of our fate, we will need a rude awakening. If this doesn't come,
then Europe, like so many other glorious civilizations, will
gradually sink into decadence without ever understanding why
or how it happened. In 1923 Spengler mused over 'The Decline
of the West'. Today we have barely time enough to comprehend
what is happening to us.

During the next few years American investment in Europe
will continue to grow far more rapidly than European investment. Its profits are already half again as large as ours. It is
taking over the major role in strategic areas of development.
This is not happening through ordinary investments, but
through actual takeovers of European firms that the Americans
then transform into rich and powerful corporations. And they
do this with European money that our own businessmen do not
know how to use.

What threatens to crush us today is not a torrent of riches,
but a more intelligent use of skills. While French, German, or
Italian firms are still groping around in the new open spaces
provided by the Treaty of Rome, afraid to emerge from the
dilapidated shelter of their old habits, American industry has
gauged the terrain and is now rolling from Naples to Amster-
dam with the ease and the speed of Israeli tanks in the Sinai
desert.

Confronted with this conquering force, European politicians
and businessmen do not know how to react. Public opinion,
confused by their contradictory statements and mysterious shifts
of policy, has no way of judging whether American investment
is good or bad.

It is both. The stimulus of competition and the introduction
of new techniques are clearly good for Europe. But the growing
underdevelopment that could transform this assistance into a
takeover is bad for us.

The danger is not in what the Americans can do, but what the
Europeans cannot do, and in the vacuum between the two. This

is why the various restrictions and prohibitions that we impose
—or would like to impose—are either irrelevant to the problem
or deal with it only peripherally. Putting an end to American
investment will not fill the vacuum; it will only weaken us
further.

While this is happening we show no signs of suffering. Our
economy grows and our standard of living rises nicely. Why
should we worry? Let's take a little look over the horizon.

CHAPTER 3

THE POST-INDUSTRIAL SOCIETY

THANKS largely to the influx of American technology and organization, Europeans are now being swept along on a tide of progress. But we have been slow to react to all this power unleashed among us. Our creative abilities are strangely paralysed, and within this general forward tide we are mired in second place—far behind the Americans.

Before analysing exactly how economic dependence slows down and limits progress, we might take a look at the future with the Hudson Institute, which has recently made a study of the world thirty years from now—the world of the next generation in the year 2000.

In 1968 Herman Kahn and the Hudson Institute published a 1,000-page report, based on current projections, of life in the year 2000.[1] Here are some of its major points.

[1] The Hudson Institute was founded by some members of the Rand Corporation. During the war Rand developed 'operational research', which for the first time made it possible to integrate all the factors involved in a strategic decision in order to clarify the available options. Its military activities were funnelled directly into the Defence Department and the White House. Although Rand's contribution was not responsible for the American military victory, which was assured one way or another, it hastened the end of the war by guaranteeing minimum loss and maximum speed for the landing operations in Europe and the Pacific.

After the war, Rand continued its operational research activities, this time on nuclear matters and the cold war. It did not assume a decision-making role, which belongs to political leaders and cannot be handled by computers. Rather, its role was to clarify and predict so that more intelligent decisions could be made.

In 1967 the nine leading powers in terms of per capita income were: the United States, Scandinavia, Canada, Germany, Britain, France, U.S.S.R., Italy, Japan.

Two other countries were also studied by the Hudson Institute—India and China. Although their per capita income is small, their future importance is very great. This makes eleven countries in all.

During the next thirty years our generation will see the advent of what Daniel Bell[2] calls the 'post-industrial society'. We should remember this term, for it is the definition of our future. It involves such fundamental changes that for certain industrialized countries life in the year 2000 will be as different from what it is today as our societies now are from Egypt or Nigeria.

In the new society, according to Bell and Kahn:

1. industrial revenue will be fifty times higher than in the pre-industrial period;
2. most economic activity will have shifted from the primary (agriculture) and secondary (industrial production) areas into the third and fourth areas (service industries, research institutes, non-profit organizations);[3]
3. private enterprise will no longer be the major source of scientific and technological development;
4. the free market will take second place to the public sector and to social services;[4]
5. most industries will be run by cybernetics;
6. the major impetus for progress will come from education and the technological innovations it utilizes;

Rand contributed to America's victory in the nuclear confrontation and the peaceful competition with Russia.

Herman Kahn and Anthony Wiener, former Rand analysts, formed a new research body called the Hudson Institute near New York City. It conducts research for the government and for private corporations.

[2] In his new book, *The Reforming of General Education*.

[3] The fourth sector is defined as a development of the third (services) which will emerge from the laws of the market and the profit system: foundations, free research, cultural and non-profit organizations, etc.

[4] In *The New Industrial State* John Kenneth Galbraith confirms this adaptation of simple market laws to more complex and controlled relationships.

7. time and space will no longer be a problem in communications;
8. the gap between high and low salaries in the post-industrial society will be considerably smaller than today.

According to this study, a country reaches the post-industrial level when per capita income exceeds $4000 a year.

Per capita income in the United States is already $3,500 a year, $1,800 in Western Europe, and $1,000 in the Soviet Union.

The following chart by Herman Kahn classifies societies according to per capita income.

TYPES OF SOCIETIES

Pre-industrial	$50 to $200 per capita
Partially industrialized or transitional	$200 to $600 per capita
Industrial	$600 to $1,500 per capita
Mass consumption or advanced industrial	$1,500 to $4,000 per capita
Post-industrial	$4,000 to $20,000 per capita

The United States and Western Europe (with Russia catching up) are both advanced industrial societies, despite obvious differences in the level, distribution, and use of income.

The Hudson Institute study goes on to show how nations are likely to be ranked thirty years from now. This serves as a useful basis for analysis.

The *post-industrial* societies will be, in this order: the United States, Japan, Canada, Sweden. That is all.[5]

The *advanced industrial* societies that have the potential to become post-industrial include: Western Europe, the Soviet Union, Israel, East Germany, Poland, Czechoslovakia, Australia, and New Zealand.

The following nations will become *consumer societies*: Mexico, Argentina, Venezuela, Chile, Colombia, South Korea, Malaysia, Formosa, and the other countries of Europe.

[5] In a colloquium in Paris in September 1967 Herman Kahn suggested, to please his audience, that France might belong to this select group. But it is no favour to 'tranquillize' us this way, for his book says just the opposite.

The rest of the world—China, India, most of South America, the Arab countries, and black Africa—will not have even reached the industrial stage.

Thus an extraordinary historical change is calmly presented to us. Within a single generation there will no longer be a difference of degree between our situation and that of the advanced countries—but a difference of kind. We will belong to a different world, a world somewhere between the advanced societies and the underdeveloped ones.

A few rare countries like Japan and Sweden, by carefully managing their resources, concentrating their talents, and adapting themselves to the demands of the new society, will manage to stay among the front runners—but not Western Europe.[6]

The purpose of our analysis, and of this book, is not to point out how shameful it would be to resign ourselves to gradual decay, but rather to find a way by which Western Europe can reverse this perilous situation and stay in the race among competing civilizations by regaining control over her own destiny.

In thirty years America will be a post-industrial society with a per capita income of $7,500. There will be only four work days a week of seven hours per day. The year will be comprised of 39 work weeks and 13 weeks of vacation. With weekends and holidays this makes 147 work days a year and 218 free days. All this within a single generation.

[6] The Japanese and Swedish models of development are quite different from one another.

CHAPTER 4

THE POWER TO CREATE

CONSIDERING the extraordinary lead enjoyed by American industry in the key sectors of our economy, some economists have asked whether the fastest path to development might not lie in letting the Americans manage our industries. In any case, this has been happening in Europe over the past few years, and there is little indication it is about to change. From an economic point of view, isn't it the simplest solution?

There is no scientific answer to this question. It may be that Europe lags so far behind in innovation and management that any attempt at economic independence would only aggravate it. But even if such a withdrawal from the fight were justified economically, we don't have to accept it. There may be political, cultural, and even moral arguments that should persuade us to reject this easy temptation to 'Americanization'. For the moment, however, we will leave the political aspect aside and concentrate on economic matters. Here we see that *independence is not an ethical notion, but an economic necessity.*

In the short run, dependence is beneficial. American investment, although it is presently an instrument of domination, is also the principal vehicle of technological progress for our economies. It introduces manufacturing processes and management techniques that are new to us. It forces European manufacturers to a rationalization and modernization they would never have agreed to without such competition. The immediate economic effect of American investment is, therefore, quite positive. If we continue to permit American investment in its present form, Europe will share in the profits that foreign investors make from their high productivity. These profits spread

27

throughout the economy, raising the general standard of living.

There is another argument for a liberal attitude towards American investments. Although an effort is being made to reorganize European production methods, with a few exceptions, a long time will pass before it is possible to offer workers the salaries paid by American firms. We ought to remember that if European industry is competitive in some areas with American industry, it is because our wage levels are only half of those in the United States.

But in the long run this will change. To ask if the Europeans should turn an increasing share of their industrial development over to the United States is like asking whether it is better to be a wage-earner or a factory owner. In any case, on the national level, considering Europe's situation today, there is a straightforward answer to this question. Economic analysis demonstrates that foreign investment imposes strict limitations on national development, limitations inherent in the very process of industrial creativity.

The American investor is willing to manufacture in Europe only those products that have already been profitable in the United States. This is a general rule based on facts we will discuss in a later chapter. By giving the Americans a dominant role in the development of new industries, we condemn ourselves to second place in the race for economic progress.

Experience consistently shows that the inventor of a new product or process has a great advantage over his rivals in a modern economy based on rapid technological change. If he agrees to share his discovery with them, he can demand high royalties in return.

For large corporations there is a direct correlation between profits and the degree of advanced research: *for the modern corporation, innovation is the major source of profit.*

Thus, the infusion of ever larger amounts of American investment in key industries has the short-term advantage of sparing Europe expensive research costs. But in the long run it deprives our economy of the ability to pursue rapid economic expansion that exists only in these key industries. The result is to reduce the profitability of exclusively European corporations, which are forced to pay increasingly high royalties for

American patents and licences. To add to this neo-colonial drain on our funds, there are the dividends that are continuously being sent back to the United States. These dividends already exceed the amount of new funds coming into Europe in the form of U.S. capital investments. This snowball phenomenon is unlikely ever to slow down of its own accord.

The long-term effect of these American investments can be compared to that of the European powers towards their former colonies. When the French built cement plants in Algeria and oil refineries in Senegal they naturally helped diversify the economies of their colonies. Even if they wanted to, these colonies could never have achieved industrial development by their own efforts because the mother country controlled the most modern areas of their economies. We can see this operating today.

But Europe is not Algeria or Senegal. If we can build a better industrial organization here in Europe, we will get faster, and considerably greater, benefits from it than we would from what American investors would leave us after they drained off dividends and royalties.

Equipping ourselves with the tools of management and organization that could make Europe an independent centre of industrial and technological creativity will be no easy task. But if we succeed, we will be able to benefit directly from the two principal sources of modern wealth: (1) technological innovation; (2) the integrated combination of production factors that is the keystone of modern business.

European governments have so far been unwilling to make this effort to catch up, and have not tried to secure the tools they need for the job. The domination of American science and industry thus continues unabated.

This kind of situation cannot go on for ever. Not the least of the risks involved is a sudden and violent reaction that could come, for example, in the form of a new political mood in Europe. 'Why don't we nationalize the American-owned firms on our soil?' some politician might suggest.

Suppose a new regime wanted to 'nationalize' IBM-France, which has several modern plants and a research laboratory at La Gaude in Provence. Having taken control of these handsome installations, the government would find that it had mistaken the shadow for the substance. What counts today for a corporation is not the walls or the machines, but the intangible elements that cannot be nationalized. Just as in biology the cell is different from the sum of its component molecules, so a modern corporation is different from the production factors that go into it. By nationalizing IBM we would simply force its managers and technicians to emigrate. We would be committing, on the scientific and strategic level, the kind of 'intellectual suicide' that Hitler's anti-Semitic policies produced in Germany thirty years ago.

This was demonstrated, in an opposite way, by Germany in 1947, when she lost most of the material forces that made her a great power. Britain, by contrast, came out of the war with most of her industry untouched. If today, twenty-six years later, Germany has overtaken Britain, it is largely because she has recovered those 'intangible' elements Britain lacked—the ability to exploit her resources and her inventiveness.

To nationalize U.S. industries in response to increased American investment is a typical reaction of an underdeveloped country, and ignores the real nature of the problem. Even if the newly nationalized firm managed to keep American-developed techniques, it would nevertheless be cut off from the flow of creative stimuli from the parent company. Within a few months it would be hopelessly out of date. Given a framework of free trade, the nationalization of American investments would simply lead to the ruin of the nationalized industries. Governments which committed such an act of folly would have to close their frontiers to shut out scientific advances made elsewhere.

Nationalization may be tempting, for it spares us the effort of thinking and seems to offer an easy answer. But it is a weapon that would only work against our own development.

Is there a less drastic course, one which a more ambitious government might take to oblige foreign investors to carry out a minimum amount of technological research in our own country? This is worth looking into, and might have some beneficial results. But we ought not to fool ourselves about the meagre advantages it would offer Europe.

An article in the *International Management Review* shows that, with a few exceptions, the distribution of power is quite different in American-owned international corporations than it is in European corporations. This difference limits the kind of restrictive measures we could take. European firms such as Philips give their foreign subsidiaries a good deal of independence. In American firms, on the other hand, the home office in the U.S. keeps tight control over every aspect of business strategy. Modern experience shows the importance of concentrating, rather than scattering, strategic decisions.

The most decisive factor in the modern economy is the combination of research with industrial infrastructure, effective means of finance, and a large scale organization. The home office of a giant corporation coordinates all of these. This means that even if American investors allow more research to be carried on in Europe, the basic source of profit for the corporations, and of technological development for the nations concerned, would still be in the place where the decisions are made—the home office in the United States.

The board of directors of a corporation uses the financial resources of its shareholders, bankers, and the capital market. It bases its judgments on assessments of its major market—which is, of course, the American market. It works, especially in large corporations, in close rapport with the government, which determines the strategy of the firm by its contracts and research grants. Also, we must not forget the importance of the intellectual environment, and particularly the relationship between the corporation and the local university.

All these elements, so tightly integrated in the structure of the modern corporation, show that the connection between the parent company in America and the European subsidiary is not governed by a simple economic law, but by a complex system of hierarchical relationships. Where there is a conflict of interest between the home office and the countries in which subsidiaries are located, obviously the home office is the boss.

Let us return a moment to the case of IBM-France, which is without question a source of wealth and progress for us. For the parent company in the United States, this subsidiary is one of many centres of research and development scattered throughout the world. Discoveries made in the laboratory at La Gaude are immediately transmitted by Telex to the United States, where the coordinating offices are located. Production programmes assigned to the French subsidiary are only a part of the global operations of a corporation whose base is in the United States.

It is over there that 'cross-fertilization' is taking place—the process that makes it possible to concentrate all the forces of research and marketing, all the implements of progress, on a single object. Economists attach a crucial importance to this process.

Even supposing that, by a policy of imposing obligatory research on American investments, Europe were able considerably to increase such programmes, she would be no less economically dependent on these investments since she would not be participating in the decision-making process. In the last analysis, it is clear that *the power to create wealth is the power to make decisions.*

The predictions of the Hudson Institute, therefore, are not unreasonable. If America is the place where decisions are made, and Europe where they are later put into application, within a single generation we will no longer belong to the same civilization. The United States will have, at least for this period of history, a monopoly on technological innovation.

There is a new society on the horizon, one which will come into being before today's thirty-year-olds go into retirement. Not only will it be a richer society, but a different kind of society, since beyond a certain level wealth is measured not so much by a higher standard of living as by a completely different way of life. The 'post-industrial society' will be distinguished by man's unprecedented freedom from physical, economic, and biological constraints. Manual labour will have virtually disappeared, there will be more leisure time than hours of work, distance will be annihilated, spectacular new methods for the diffusion of culture and information will be developed, and we will enjoy a vastly increased new power over nature and life. Will this be a happier society? That is another question to which we have no answer. But it is certain that this society will be the avant-garde of human history, and that is what concerns us.

By extrapolating present trends, it seems clear that we Europeans cannot hope to participate fully in that world of the future. This does not mean we will be poor; probably we will grow even richer. But we will be overtaken and dominated, for the first time in our history, by a more advanced civilization.

These scientific forecasts do not describe a certainty, but a probability we are still free to change. This is particularly true because wealth and power are no longer measured in material terms. They are not gifts of nature or chance, like oil, or gold, or even population. Rather they are victories won by the human spirit: the ability to transform an idea into a reality through the industrial process; the talent for coordinating skills and making rigid organizations flexible. Does Europe lack the wellsprings of these skills?

The know-how that opens the gate to the post-industrial society can exist only in an independent community, for the community where strategic industrial decisions are made is the community that will break through barriers, occupy forward positions, and hold the reins of power.

What we need to put us back into the race is organizational skill and a determination to be independent. To understand what this involves, let's look at the American technostructure in action.

PART 2

AMERICA'S ARSENAL

CHAPTER 5

THE AMERICAN COLOSSUS

WHAT we are faced with is not classic imperialism driven by a desire for conquest, but an overflow of power due to the difference in 'pressure' between America and the rest of the world. America's enormous power is widely felt, but little understood. It has been written about everywhere, yet it changes so quickly that descriptions are soon out of date. Here are a few examples of America's place in the world.

American industry produces twice the goods and services of all European industry combined—including both Britain and the Common Market—and two and a half times more than the Soviet Union, which has a greater population than the U.S. It produces a third of the total production of all other countries in the world. The Americans have achieved this with only 7 per cent of the surface of the globe and 6 per cent of its population.

One-third of all students in the world pursuing a higher education are American. The number of students, as compared to the total population, is double that of any other country.[1] For every 1,000 inhabitants there are 29 Americans studying at a university, 18 Russians, 10 Dutchmen, and 10 Swedes.

All by themselves the Americans consume a third of the total world production of energy, and have one-third of all the world's highways. Half the passenger miles flown every year are by American airlines. Two trucks of every five on the road are American-made and American-based. Americans own three out of every five automobiles in the world.

[1] Such a gap makes it possible to disregard the differences in the age pyramid in certain countries, as well as varying definitions of who is a 'student'.

Advanced technology and management skills have raised per capita production in the United States to a level 40 per cent above that of Sweden (next highest), 60 per cent above Germany, 70 per cent above France, and 80 per cent above Britain. The driving force behind this power is American business. The combined profits of the ten biggest firms in France, Britain, and Germany (30 in all) is $2 billion. The profits of General Motors alone are $2·25 billion.[2] To equal the profits of General Motors you would have to add the ten leading Japanese firms to the European total. These 40 firms employ 3·5 million people, while General Motors employs 730,000—or about a fifth.

From 1961 to 1966 American corporations doubled the annual total of their investments. They did this in large part out of their earnings rather than from bank loans. In France, on the other hand, the growth rate of investments was about half that in the U.S., and the amount financed by earnings has continually decreased (less than 60 per cent in 1966).

During the past six years the gross profits of American corporations have grown each year. As a percentage of gross national production (GNP) they were:

1961	7·7 per cent
1962	8·0 per cent
1963	8·3 per cent
1964	8·8 per cent
1965	9·1 per cent
1966	9·5 per cent

By comparison, the gross profits of French firms (as a percentage of GNP) have continuously fallen—from 6·6 per cent in 1961 to 3·5 per cent in 1966—and there are worse performers than France in Europe.

This explains why the role of American industry has become even more powerful than it was ten years ago. The latest figures (1966) show that among all firms doing more than a billion dollars of business a year, 60 are in the United States and only 27 are not American-owned. North America has more than twice as many of these industrial giants, with their capacity for fast commercial and technological development, as the rest of

[2] *Fortune (August 1966).*

the world combined.[3] This remarkable growth also has important social side-effects, as is indicated below:

SCALE OF INCOME IN THE UNITED STATES
(by family per year)

	1950	1960	1965
	per cent	per cent	per cent
Over $10,000	7	18	25
$10,000 to $7,000	13	21	24
$7,000 to $5,000	20	22	18
$5,000 to $3,000	30	19	16
Under $3,000	30	20	17

Thus in 1950, 60 per cent of all American families earned less than $5,000 a year, and 7 per cent earned more than $10,000. By 1965 the number of families earning less than $5,000 dropped to 33 per cent, while 25 per cent earned more than $10,000. We will keep these figures in mind for the moment without going into detail, precisely because they lie at the heart of our discussion. And, also so far as this book is concerned, so that the relationship between equity and growth may remain an open subject.

[3] Of the 27 firms that are not American-owned, 12 are German, 6 British, 3 Dutch, 2 Japanese, 2 French, 1 Italian, and 1 Swiss.

CHAPTER 6

THE GROWTH SPIRAL

As Octave Gelinier has shown, the 'secret of effective competition' does not depend entirely upon the size of a firm.[1] Some mergers only multiply structural or management defects. But in general, the largest corporations are the ones most likely to undertake the investment and research activities essential to successful competition—particularly in fields of advanced technology. The example furnished by these firms is worth looking into.

From 1961–1965, the last period for which complete figures are available, both the United States and the European Economic Community enjoyed a favourable growth rate, thus making for a more homogeneous comparison. We will look first at changes in *size*, then examine the financial *structure* and *results*—which are more important.

Corporations whose annual revenues exceeded $500 million in 1961 were located as follows:

United States	97
European Community	27
Rest of the world	22

while five years later:

United States	134
European Community	41
Rest of the world	49

Although there was a slight improvement for Europe during

[1] Octave Gelinier has written two important books on modern capitalism: *Morale de l'entreprise et destin de la nation* and *Le Secret des structures compétitives.*

40

this period, American firms outnumbered those of the Community by nearly four to one—even though population was roughly equivalent. Now let us consider the environment in which these corporations have been operating.

The increasing number of mergers in Europe has aggravated the imbalance of European industry. Our industry has always been marked by a relatively small number of medium-sized firms with sales between $250 and $500 million. In this category U.S. firms outnumber European firms six to one.

Obviously the fabric of European industry is being stretched thin, and if mergers continue under present haphazard conditions, we will have a few global corporations and a great number of tradition-bound small businesses unable to meet outside competition. These mergers have left a vacuum that so far is unfilled.

A second weakness results from the fact that the growth rate of sales for large European corporations is considerably less than that of their American rivals, as the table indicates:

GROSS REVENUE OF LARGE CORPORATIONS

(over $300 million a year)

	1961	1965	Per cent
	(in billions of dollars)		of change
European Community	31·5	42·9	+36
United States	157·6	220·1	+40

World sales of large corporations have thus increased by 40 per cent in the U.S. and 36 per cent in Europe. This gap is growing. Further, these figures are distorted by price increases which have not been the same on both sides of the Atlantic. While the index of wholesale industrial prices remained steady in the United States during this period, they rose 10 per cent in the Common Market. Thus the real growth rate of the Community was 26 or 28 per cent against 40 per cent in the United States. American firms have grown one-third again as fast as ours.

This relative decline of economic strength is illustrated by the following table by the Compagnie Lambert of Brussels:

SHARE OF WORLD PRODUCTION

Area	U.S.	Common Market	Rest of world
Machinery	70 per cent	13 per cent	17 per cent
Autos	76 „	13 „	11 „
Oil	73 „	14 „	13 „
Electronics	68 „	15 „	17 „
Chemicals	62 „	21 „	17 „

Computers are the most technologically advanced area, and Christopher Layton[2] has worked out the following table of firms installing their products in Europe during 1965:

IBM	62 per cent
ICT (British)	9 „
Bull (French)	7 „
Olivetti (Italian)	2 „
Others (mostly British)	20 „

Since the computer sections of both Bull and Olivetti have now been taken over by General Electric, the American share of the European market is thus 71 per cent.

There is, however, something more important than mere size —the financial *structure* of these firms and their *profits*.

First, financial structure. In France, Germany, and Italy there are few firms with equity capital exceeding $50 million. During the last year for which figures are available there were only 95, as compared to 440 in the United States—or five times more. The total capital held by these American corporations was $150 billion, or ten times the combined capital of the largest corporations in the three leading countries of the Common Market. This means that each American firm has twice the capital assets of a comparable European firm.

Because of this weakness in its financial structure, European

[2] In *Transatlantic Investment* (1966).

industry has not been able to obtain the funds it needs on the European capital market—particularly since European governments and American firms investing in Europe drain funds from the same capital market. There has been almost no increase in the amount of common stocks issued within the European Community. This shortage of capital has put European firms in a delicate situation, either pushing them further into debt, or preventing them from expanding. Borrowing intensifies their problem, for their ability to finance investment out of future earnings is compromised by mounting interest charges on their loans.

A study of 200 French firms showed that medium and long-term debt rose by 14 per cent a year, or 70 per cent in a four-year period. In Italy debt has risen by 16 per cent a year; in Germany by 12 per cent. The result is the *deterioration of net profit margins* during the past few years. For large corporations the net profit margins are:

CHANGES IN PROFIT MARGINS IN RELATION TO SALES

	1961	1965
Common Market	3·42 per cent	3·01 per cent
United States	6·05 per cent	7·09 per cent

The mean profit margin went down by nearly half a point for European firms during this period, and even further in 1966 and 1967, although we do not yet have complete figures. During the same period it grew by more than a full percentage point for American firms. There figures are of *crucial importance*. They show that in the global competition for markets European firms are finding it harder and harder to stay in the running.

The first of the following unpublished tables by the Compagnie Lambert shows gross sales for the major American and European firms in chemicals, electronics, and automobiles, and the percentage of net profit for the most recent year available; the second table shows the amounts set aside by each firm for internal financing—that is, for investment and for growth.

America's Arsenal

GROSS SALES AND PROFITS

Area	Company	Gross sales in billions of dollars	Net profit as per cent of gross sales
CHEMICALS	DuPont de Nemours (U.S.)	3·02	13·5
	Union Carbide (U.S.)	2·06	11·0
	Monsanto (U.S.)	1·47	8·4
	Dow Chemical (U.S.)	1·18	9·2
	ICI (Britain)	2·28	9·1
	Bayer (Germany)	1·58	4·2
	Hoechst (Germany)	1·31	4·9
	Rhone-Poulenc (France)	1·01	2·2
	Badische Anilin (Germany)	1·01	7·0
ELECTRICAL AND ELECTRONICS	General Electric U.S.)	6·21	5·7
	IBM (U.S.)	3·57	13·4
	Western Electric (U.S.)	3·36	5·0
	Westinghouse (U.S.)	2·39	4·5
	RCA (U.S.)	2·04	4·9
	General Telephone (U.S.)	2·04	8·2
	Philips (Holland)	2·08	5·3
	Siemens (Germany)	1·79	2·5
	AEG (Germany)	1·03	2·4
	Bosch (Germany)	·74	1·3
AUTOS	GM (U.S.)	2,125	850
	Ford (U.S.)	11·50	6·1
	Chrysler (U.S.)	5·30	4·4
	American Motors (U.S.)	·99	·5
	Volkswagen (Germany)	2·32	4·0
	Fiat (Italy)	1·53	2·5
	British Motors (Britain)	1·35	3·3
	Daimler-Benz (Germany)	1·30	3·0
	Citroën (France)	·79	·7

PROFITS AND INVESTMENT FROM PROFITS

Area	Company	Net profit (in millions of dollars)	Investment from profits (in millions of dollars)
CHEMICALS	Du Pont de Nemours (U.S.)	407	162
	Union Carbide (U.S.)	226	90
	Monsanto (U.S.)	123	49
	Dow Chemical (U.S.)	108	43
	ICI (Britain)	208	83
	Bayer (Germany)	86	67
	Hoechst (Germany)	64	26
	Rhone-Poulenc (France)	22	9
	Badische Anilin (Germany)	71	28
ELECTRICAL AND ELECTRONICS	General Electric (U.S.)	355	142
	IBM (U.S.)	476	190
	Western Electric (U.S.)	168	68
	Westinghouse (U.S.)	107	43
	RCA (U.S.)	101	40
	General Telephone (U.S.)	166	66
	Philips (Holland)	110	44
	Siemens (Germany)	45	18
	AEG (Germany)	25	10
	Bosch (Germany)	10	4
AUTOS	GM (U.S.)	20·70	10·3
	Ford (U.S.)	703	281
	Chrysler (U.S.)	233	93
	American Motors (U.S.)	5	2
	Volkswagen (Germany)	94	38
	Fiat (Italy)	39	16
	British Motors (Britain)	45	18
	Daimler-Benz (Germany)	39	16
	Citroën (France)	6	2

Economists believe that net profits should be 12 to 13 per cent of equity capital in order to maintain growth in areas of advanced technology. This is normal for big business in

America, where the profit ratio sometimes goes as high as 30 per cent. According to the latest figures, the profit ratio in France in 1966 was barely 4 per cent, and the European average only 5 per cent. This was less than the general interest rate, and explains why European business has so little attraction for the average investor.

If, as we have seen, financial strength of a corporation is a key factor in development, the level of investment in technological research is equally important, for innovation has now become the key weapon in competition. The famous economist Schumpeter predicted this even before the war when he wrote: 'The really crucial competition will be in new goods and new techniques. This competition will exact a decisive advantage in cost and quality, and strike not only at the profit margins and production figures of corporations, but at *their foundations and their very existence.*'

Several studies deal with this new kind of industrial warfare.[3] The development of new products has hit a momentum undreamed of before the war, or even ten years ago. The U.S. chemical industry, for example, now considers it normal that half its business is based on products that didn't exist ten years ago.

If innovation has become the modern form of competition, the amount of money a corporation devotes to research and development is absolutely crucial. American leadership in this area is overwhelming. In 1965, the last year for which figures are available, the Americans devoted 3·61 per cent of their national product to research and development, as against 2·01 per cent for the Europeans. Predictions for 1970 are even more dramatic, for they show that research will rise to 4·6 per cent in the United States as against 2·5 per cent in Europe.

Research and development expenses during the most recent year for which we have figures were $94 per capita in the U.S. compared to $25 in Europe. The Americans spent a total of $17 billion and the Common Market countries only $3 billion. A comparison of research budgets of the largest chemical firms in the U.S. and Europe, as shown in the table below, is particu-

[3] Particularly the American travel notes of Pierre Cognard, representative to the DGRST (Délégation Générale à la Recherche Scientifique et Technique), and the Lambert report for 1966.

larly dramatic, since chemicals is the one area where Europe still remains competitive with the United States.

ANNUAL RESEARCH EXPENDITURES IN THE CHEMICAL INDUSTRY

Company	Research expenditures (in millions of dollars)
Du-Pont de Nemours (U.S.)	110
Union Carbide (U.S.)	78
International Harvester (U.S.)	64
Hoechst (Europe)	64
Bayer (Europe)	60
Badische Anilin (Europe)	54

Research expenditures not only speed up the pace of scientific discovery, but *shorten* the gap between the laboratory and the production line. This is the fundamental mark of the modern economy. This time lag between the scientific invention and the manufacture of the item was:

112 years for photography (1727–1839)
56 years for the telephone (1820–1876)
35 years for radio (1867–1902)
15 years for radar (1925–1940)
12 years for television (1922–1934)
6 years for the atomic bomb (1939–1945)
5 years for the transistor (1948–1953)
3 years for the integrated circuit (1958–1961)

It is in this perspective that competition by the creation of new products assumes the importance described by Schumpeter. Only those firms capable of developing and maintaining their technological leadership will continue to grow. As Cognard concluded after his visit to the United States:

'Independent of their industrial potential, American firms seem to have done a better job than we in figuring out new scientific possibilities from the mass of data that determine the expansion of a firm and its markets. With the help of computers, which simplify problems of coordination, a direct relationship has now been worked out between laboratory data, production problems, and marketing forecasts—all of which help give the firm a comprehensive view of the problems involved ... Accustomed to work in technical fields which pose far broader problems than those of the commercial market, and aided by government contracts, American firms are now developing industrial and technological methods far advanced over anything in Europe.'

A new factor in the equation is the growing, and already predominant, role of the federal government in key industries. This is not generally understood in Europe, although federal agencies have been collaborating with American corporations in developing advanced technology ever since the end of the war. According to the National Science Foundation the government pays the following part of research expenses in different areas of industry:

GOVERNMENT ROLE IN DEFENCE EXPENDITURES

Industries	Research expenditures (in billions of dollars)	Part financed by the government
Aviation and spacecraft	3·96	90 per cent
Electrical and electronic	2·38	65 per cent
Scientific instruments	·39	42 per cent
Machinery	·93	31 per cent
Metallurgical alloys	·11	28 per cent
Chemicals	1·10	20 per cent

This table shows that federal spending is crucial in certain areas such as transport, communications, and electronics—the areas of future growth.

Cognard has studied two electronics firms, one French, one American:

COMPARISON OF A FRENCH ELECTRONICS FIRM WITH A
SIMILAR AMERICAN FIRM

	Annual sales (in millions of dollars)	Annual research expenses	Amount financed by government
French firm	$1·7	$·08 ($80,000)	$ ·016 ($16,000)
American firm	$23·0	$2·0	$ 1·2
Relationship between the two firms	13·5	25	75

Thus for two similar firms, the ratio of sales is 13 to 1, of research 25 to 1, and of government-aided research 75 to 1. This shows how benefits multiply for firms that have gone beyond the threshold and are able to engage in joint projects.

We can now see the elements of this vigorous growth process that characterizes today's America:

1. Great size permits the development of an advanced technology;
2. This scientific potential pushes the firm into new areas and thereby places it in a position of leadership;
3. The firm becomes useful to the government for carrying out various projects, and wins government contracts and tax-supported research grants;
4. This in turn increases its profit potential and its growth— the circle becomes a self-generating spiral.

Beyond this first line of explanation, observers' intuition and, more recently, scientific investigation have uncovered a second level that may be the base of this spiral of progress we have been describing. The factors that make for economic success would not be able to develop and *combine* if there were not a favourable environment. Without trying to analyse the soil that nourishes American business—which would go beyond the scope of this book—we can sketch in its hazy, but still visible, outlines.

Behind the success story of American industry there lies the talent for accepting and manoeuvring change. Technological advance comes from virtuosity in management. Both are due to lightning strides in education. There is no miracle at work here. America is now reaping a staggering profit from the most profitable investment of all—the education of its citizens. This is the story told by the documents we are now going to look at.

CHAPTER 7

THE DENISON REPORT

ONLY recently have there been attempts to make a theoretical analysis of the modern factors of productivity. Edward F. Denison, who wrote his doctoral thesis in 1964 while connected with the National Council on Economic Development, has made a major contribution in this field. His is the first systematic study of the origins of American economic expansion.

Under the influence of this study, the Department of Statistics of the U.S. Bureau of the Census has recently compiled statistics illustrating this process of expansion. From now on, the Bureau of the Census will publish a yearly report on 'long-term economic expansion.' What are Denison's findings, as backed up by the Bureau of the Census?

For years economists have spoken about the factors of expansion only in the most general terms. Until quite recently, even in the United States, they were not particularly interested in discovering its sources or methods for stimulating it.

The debate was launched in 1776, nearly 200 years ago, by Adam Smith in *The Wealth of Nations*. Throughout the nineteenth century his successors were concerned primarily with such problems as price levels and the allocation of resources. In the twentieth century, under the influence of John Maynard Keynes, economists have been preoccupied by business cycles and ways to avoid depressions—which they did successfully after the Second World War. Only today are they beginning to undertake a systematic study of the forces that stimulate and sustain long-term expansion.

In the early part of this century, expansion was basically a question of numbers: according to Denison more than half of economic development in the period 1909–1929 was due to the expansion of the *labour force* and the growth of *invested capital*. After the Depression this was no longer true. Between 1929 and 1957 these quantitative factors (labour and capital) were responsible for only a third of the increase in gross national product. Today the most important factors in economic expansion are *education and technological innovation*.

Julius Shiskin, head of the statistics division of the U.S. Bureau of the Census, says that a two-year study by his office confirms Denison's theories. The Census Bureau's graphs reinforce Denison's conviction that the labour force has played a minor role in recent American economic expansion. During the first part of the century, until 1929, the number of man-hours grew by 1·1 per cent, while in the period from 1929 to 1957 they decreased by ·2 per cent. These figures do not include man-hours in government, and therefore should be modified. But it is clear that the decrease in the number of work hours per man in the industrial area of the economy has cut down the growth rate. Denison places this reduction at ·3 per cent. It would have been considerably more if it had not been offset by increased productivity. Obviously it is not labour that is responsible for expansion.

Invested capital, on the other hand, grew by 2·6 per cent a year from 1912 to 1929, and during the following period (until 1957) industrial plant and equipment increased by about 50 per cent. Denison estimates that capital investment accounted for 23 per cent of economic expansion during the first period, and only 15 per cent during the second (1929–1957) period. It is not the growth of invested capital that explains the new phase of modern growth.

Recent economic expansion is basically due to dramatic increases in productivity. At the beginning of the century, productivity per man-hour in the private industrial sector grew by 1·6 per cent a year; since then it has been growing by 2·7 per cent a year. But it is not enough to say that productivity is increasing. The important thing is to find out exactly what controls the relationship between the quantity of productive factors used (men and capital), and the production that results, between what is invested and what is produced—that is, productivity.

The major conclusion of the Denison report is that *education is the most important factor*, and it is at the very top of his list of factors of economic expansion. He calculates that education accounted for 11 per cent of economic growth in the first third of the century, for 23 per cent in the period 1929–1957, and for even more since then.

Statistics compiled by the Bureau of the Census testify to the extraordinary development of education in the United States. In 1930 the total sum spent on education in America was $3·2 billion; by 1965 it had multiplied more than ten times to $39 billion. In 1900 only 4 per cent of Americans of university age were enrolled; by 1965 that figure had increased ten times, and is now 44 per cent. Further, the average number of school years completed by 25-year-olds rose from 8 years in 1910 to 12 years in 1965.

If the diffusion of education is now, according to Denison's theory, the primary factor in economic development, the second is what he calls the 'growth of knowledge'—the enrichment of education and its expansion to include adults, making the new technology available to them. It is clearly impossible to make a statistic out of the growth of knowledge, but we can measure that part of it which includes expenditures on research and development. The Bureau of the Census has assembled a chart from three separate sources, which shows that money spent on research and development, on the 'growth of knowledge', rose from $166 million in 1930 to $19 billion in 1964—more than a hundredfold increase.

There is a delightful little Chinese poem, less dry than Denison's report and much older, that could also serve as a formula for American expansion. As Kuan-tzu said twenty-six centuries ago:

If you plan for a year, plant a seed.
If for ten years, plant a tree.
If for a hundred years, teach the people.
If you plant a seed once, you will reap one harvest.
If you plant a tree, you will reap ten harvests.
If you teach the people, you will reap a hundred harvests.

Or as Kuan-tzu said with even greater economy:

If you give a man a fish, he will have a single meal.
If you teach him how to fish, he will eat all his life.

Working from Denison's theory about the importance of education, two other scholars have made a comparative study of the United States and other industrialized countries. The study by Dimitri Chorafas[1] of the University of Washington covers twenty-four countries; that by the Frenchman, Raymond Poignant, together with the Dutchman, Kohnstamm, is the first complete comparative study of education in nine developed countries (the United States, the six Common Market nations, Britain, and the Soviet Union).

They show that France, pushed by unprecedented population growth, has made great strides. Between 1950 and 1960 the percentage of new teachers in France has been the highest in the world: a 126-per-cent-increase for secondary school teachers, and 102 per cent for teachers in *lycées*—against a 75 per cent increase in the United States and 56 per cent in the USSR. For university professors the French growth rate is also the highest: an increase of 131 per cent, against 58 per cent in the United States, 57 per cent in Britain, and 63 per cent in the USSR.

This increase in the number of teachers has obviously been accompanied by an increase in the number of students, but not enough to bring France—which leads Western Europe—up to the level we need. In this respect, the chart by professor Chorafas is instructive:

EDUCATION
(from the Chorafas report)

Country	Number of students in 1966	As percentage of the population from 20 to 24
United States	5,526,000	43 per cent
USSR	4,000,000	24 ,,
Japan	1,370,000	13·5 ,,
France	500,000	16 ,,
Italy	284,000	6·9 ,,
Germany	280,000	7·5 ,,
Canada	230,000	22·5 ,,
Britain	165,000	4·8 ,,
Sweden	62,000	11 ,,
Belgium	54,000	10 ,,

[1] *Brain Gain or Brain Drain.*

France and the rest of Europe are far behind the United States, where 43 per cent of people between 20 and 24 are enrolled in colleges and universities. In the Soviet Union the figure is 24 per cent; while in Europe it varies between 16 and 7 per cent. Britain is in the worst position—which, according to Denison, explains a great deal about the current stagnation of British development despite a strong industrial base.

During the most recent year for which figures are available, 101,000 people graduated from college in the Common Market countries (180 million population) as against 450,000 in the United States, with nearly the same population (190 million). America had four times as many graduates as the Common Market countries.

Looking at it by fields of study, the situation is even clearer, especially in science and technology. In the Common Market there were 25,000 graduates with degrees in science, or 1·1 per cent of those in their age group. In the United States there were 78,000 graduates in science, or 3·9 per cent of those in their age group. Thus the United States is producing scientists and engineers three times faster than the Common Market.

Finally, these reports show what chance children of manual labourers and less fortunate elements of the population have for higher education. In France, workers[2] form 56 per cent of the population, but their children represent only 12·6 per cent of the students. The same is true in other Common Market countries: 11·5 per cent for Belgium, 10 per cent in Holland, and 7·5 per cent in Germany. In the United States, on the other hand, from *three to five times as many children of workers and farmers have access to higher education than in the Common Market countries.*

Poignant concludes: 'Looking at access to higher education from a social point of view, it is clear that the Common Market countries, individually and together, offer the least opportunity to children in the lower income groups for higher education.' By projecting Denison's theory of expansion, this could easily explain American pre-eminence in the most advanced areas of science and industry. This is where all the elements come together: equity and efficiency, education and mobility, the mechanics of progress. In the last part of this book we will try

[2] Including farmers.

to return to these theses, for they can save us from fatalism and a failure of nerve.

But right now what we have to worry about is that we may never catch up unless we change the structure of our societies. As Poignant ends his report: 'The situation of the Common Market countries, from the viewpoint of "human capital" of highly qualified personnel, will be worse in 1970 and 1975 than it was in 1950 and 1960.'

The growing 'technological gap' between America and Europe is due primarily to a relative weakness of science and research—which stems from the lack of higher education. But it is also due to an apparent inability, resulting from a refusal to invest in human beings, to utilize modern methods of management.

One of the leading experts on this subject, Robert S. Mc-Namara, who reorganized the U.S. Defense Department, after having revolutionized the automobile industry, gave his views on this subject at a seminar in Jackson, Mississippi.

CHAPTER 8

McNAMARA ON THE 'GAP'

Excerpts from remarks by Robert McNamara at Millsaps College, Jackson, Mississippi, 27 February 1967.

IN the modern world, national defence and security are based on economic and scientific development. This is sometimes difficult for us to understand, since we have some stereotyped views which translate security into a purely military term. Security has, of course, a military component. But we make a dangerous and myopic mistake to believe that security and military power are synonymous.

History is full of human folly. And surely one of the most foolish features of man all through history is his almost incurable insistence on spending more energy and wealth on waging war than in preventing it.

It has not proved to be a very good bargain.

We read a great deal today about the crisis of the economic gap between the underdeveloped countries of Asia, Africa and Latin America, and the more favoured nations of the Northern hemisphere.

The average annual per capita income in some 40 of the world's poorest countries today is roughly $120. That is less than 35c a day. The annual per capita income in the United States is nearly $3,000. That is almost $8·00 a day. That is a difference of 2,000 per cent.

This is no mere economic gap. It is a seismic fissure, driving deep into the earth's sociological crust to a certain, if hidden, fault line. It can produce—and it *will* produce—thunderous earthquakes of violence if rich and poor countries alike do not do more to meet the threat.

But seismic sociological explosions are much more damaging and deadly than natural volcanic explosions—and the real difference between them is that the former can be predicted.

Not only can they be predicted theoretically, they can often be practically prevented.

Let us be blunt. If the wealthy nations of the world do not do more to close this sundering economic split which cleaves the abundant northern half of the planet from the hungering southern hemisphere, none of us will ultimately be secure.

The seismic social shocks will reach us all—and with them will come the inevitable tidal waves of violence. The economic chaos that is foreseeable when we are faced with such disparity is as threatening to the security of the United States as Chinese nuclear weapons. It is as simple and as sobering as that.

Now, let me say a word about the second gap.

Unlike the first one, this second gap is between the *developed* nations: specifically between the highly industrialized nations of Europe, and ourselves.

The Europeans have termed it the Technological Gap. Their complaint is that we are so surpassing them in industrial development that we will eventually create a kind of technological colonialism.

Prime Minister Harold Wilson of Great Britain used some rather pointed language at a recent meeting of the Council of Europe at Strasbourg. He warned of 'an industrial helotry under which we in Europe produce only the conventional apparatus of a modern economy, while becoming increasingly dependent on American business for the sophisticated apparatus which will call the industrial tune in the 70's and 80's.'

And at the last meeting, in Paris, of the Atlantic Pact, the subject that dominated the debates was this technological gap. It is the major problem of our time; but I believe that the technological gap is misnamed. It is not so much a technological gap as it is a managerial gap. And the brain drain occurs not merely because we have more advanced technology here in the United States but rather because we have more modern and effective management.

God is clearly democratic. He distributes brain power universally. But He quite justifiably expects us to do something efficient and constructive with that priceless gift. That is what management is all about. Management is, in the end, the most creative of all the arts—for its medium is human talent itself.

What, in the end, is management's most fundamental task? It is to deal with change. Management is the gate through which social, political, economic and technological change—indeed, change in every dimension—is rationally and effectively spread through society.

Some critics, today, keep worrying that our democratic, free societies are becoming over-managed. The real truth is precisely the opposite. As paradoxical as it may sound, the real threat to democracy comes from under-management, not from over-management. Society cannot survive and develop unless management continues to make progress.

The under-organization, the under-management of a society is not the respect of liberty. It is simply to let some force other than reason shape reality. That force may be unbridled emotion. It may be greed, it may be aggressiveness, it may be hatred, it may be ignorance, it may be inertia, it may be anything *other* than reason. But whatever it is, if it is *not* reason that rules man, then man falls short of his potential.

Vital decision-making, in policy matters as well as in business, must remain at the top. That is partly—though not completely—what the top is for. But rational decision-making depends on having a full range of rational options from which to choose. Successful management organizes the enterprise so that this process can best take place. It is a mechanism whereby free men can most efficiently exercise their reason, initiative, creativity and personal responsibility.

This is the great human adventure of our time. And to create the necessary organization for a precise formulation of the different options which underlie our decisions is an exalting adventure. All reality can be reasoned about. And *not to* quantify, classify, measure what can be dealt with in this way is only to be content with something less than the full range of reason.

The argument against modern tools like the computer is, in the end, an argument against reason itself. Not that a computer is a substitute for reason. Quite the contrary, it is the product of reason and it assists us in the application of reason.

But to argue that some phenomena transcend precise

measurement—which is true enough—is no excuse for neglecting the arduous task of carefully analysing what *can* be measured.

A computer does not substitute for judgment any more than a pencil substitutes for literacy. But writing ability without a pencil is not a particular advantage.

Modern creative management of huge, complex phenomena is impossible without both the technical equipment and the technical skill which the advance of human knowledge has brought us.

In my view, the industrial gap that is beginning to widen between Europe and the United States is due precisely to what we have been discussing here.

Now, how can that gap be closed?

Ultimately, it can be closed only at its origin: education.

Europe is weak educationally. And that weakness is seriously crippling its growth. It is weak in its general education; it is weak in its technical education, and it is particularly weak in its managerial education.

In the United Kingdom, France, Germany and Italy, about 90 per cent of the 13 and 14-year-old students are enrolled in school. But after age 15, there is a tremendous drop-off. Then, less than 20 per cent remain in school.

In the United States, 95 per cent of all the 13 and 14-year-olds are in school. But what is more important is that at age 18 we still have more than 45 per cent pursuing their education. We have more than 4 million students in college, and this represents some 40 per cent of our college-age population. In Western Europe this percentage ranges between 65 per cent and 15 per cent. But what is also to the point is that modern managerial education, for private enterprise as well as government, is almost unknown in industrialized Europe.

Technological advance has two bedrock requisites: broad general knowledge, and modern managerial competence. It cannot come into being without improving the foundation of it all, which is education of the young, as well as adults. If Europe really wants to close the technological gap, it has to improve its education, both general and special, and both quantitatively and qualitatively. There is just no other way to get to the fundamental root of the problem.

Science and technology, and modern management, do not sum up the entire worth of education. Developing our human capabilities to the fullest is what ultimately matters most. Call it humanism or call it whatever you like, but that is clearly what education in the final analysis is all about.

But without modern science and technology—and the generalist and managerial infrastructure to go with it—progress of any kind, spiritual, humanistic, economic or otherwise, will become increasingly less possible everywhere in the world.

Without this kind of progress, that is, without progress in education, the world is simply going to remain explosively backward, unbalanced and provincial.

CHAPTER 9

AMERICA IN 1980

IN Chapter 6 we spoke of a 'spiral of progress'; a technological breakthrough, an expansion of dimensions, a collaboration between the corporation, the government, and the university, the cross-fertilization of research, new growth, etc. Now we are going to look at the launching of a *second spiral*, even greater than the first.

Denison and McNamara both agree that continuing education is the driving force behind technological innovation. In the next stage this is going to revolutionize methods of gaining and spreading knowledge, of storing and transmitting information. The widespread use of intelligence aids has given the American economy a new surge forward which will push it into the post-industrial society. We have tried to look over the horizon to the year 2000. Now let's look more seriously at an intermediary stage: America in 1980.

This date, only a few years away,[1] has been the object of numerous studies, all of which arrive at the same conclusion: the second industrial revolution, symbolized by the computer, will be the synthesis of intellectual progress and economic growth, of thought fused with power.

General Electric has joined with Time, Inc., and American Telephone and Telegraph with the *Reader's Digest* to form companies to carry out research in new methods of learning, communication, and invention. They intend to satisfy the needs not of science-fiction readers, but of investors. The president of

[1] Fifteen years is no longer the usual limit for 'intellectual speculation', but for 'industrial programming' for large corporations holding government contracts.

62

the General Learning Corporation, a research branch of General Electric, has released a study of 'the major problems of society in the year 1980.' This is what it means for the United States.[2]

In no other period of history has our way of life, our institutions, our whole society been so completely subject to change. This rapid rate of change is likely to increase during the next decade. The three most important aspects of our social environment in 1980 will be:

1. Near-total urbanization;
2. Automation of industry;
3. A revolution in communications media.

Taken together these three factors will bring about a new form of social organization. Urbanization, automation, and communications have different effects, but react upon one another. We should look at them as convergent forces that will create a new society—the society of the second industrial revolution.

The first industrial revolution is less than a century old. It was a mechanical revolution that transformed Europe and North America. Railroads opened up our continents; industrialization and urbanization brought about extensive social changes. Mass production and the internal combustion engine have had a radical and continuing effect on our lives. Traditional farm life is gradually dying out, while the private automobile has transformed society, our way of life, and our methods of education. Our society today, essentially urban and industrial, has many problems to resolve, but it also has a brilliant future.

In looking at this future, we see a continuing growth of the cities that will lead to a near-total urbanization of the industrial world. The following chart shows the predicted growth of world population and the growth curve of the urban population. The prognosis is clear.

[2] Report by Richard Shetler and Tom O. Paine (General Electric, California) and Alex Groner (Time, Inc., New York).

WORLD URBANIZATION

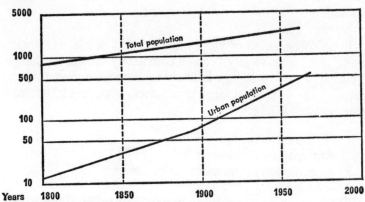

The rewards of urban life are considerable. The second chart shows the relation between urban population and per capita income. The lure of higher salaries attracts a growing number

INCOME AND URBANIZATION

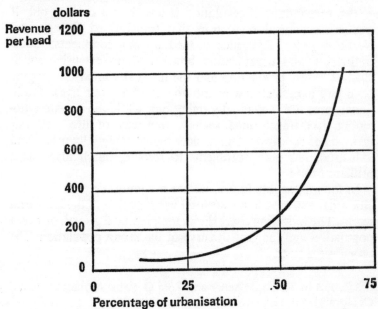

of people to the cities. But urban life requires a high level of technical and intellectual skills. This stimulates demands for better general education.

While cities in America and Western Europe are growing rapidly, those in other parts of the world are growing even faster. Projections of urbanization in the underdeveloped countries of Africa, Asia, and Latin America show high growth rates for the remainder of this century. This growth will be accompanied by rising demands for better education, since education can be translated into higher incomes.

Expenditures on education, already high in many of these countries, will multiply, thereby posing new demands that can be met only by greatly increased Western aid. This will require new systems of education—perhaps the most urgent demand of all. Fifty years ago, in *The War of the Worlds*, H. G. Wells foresaw a 'dramatic race between education and catastrophe.' We still cannot be sure how this race will turn out.

It took the United States a century to become an intellectually equipped society. It was hard in the beginning, universal education was often inefficient and always expensive. But one way or another, the problem now has been mastered. However, while we are still dealing with old problems that are far from being resolved in our own country, new conditions are arising that we must adapt ourselves to.

One of the most important developments in the United States during the next 30 years will be the steady reduction of the work week—a reduction that will be intensified by automation.[3] During the past 50 years the average work week has been slashed in half by mechanization. The worker today is better educated and somewhat older when he enters the labour force. He works shorter hours, has more holidays, and retires younger. These changes are having an enormous impact on the whole system of education.

Workers already have more time to do the things they enjoy. Since their preferences often reflect their level of education, more free time will impose even greater burdens on our educational system. Also, technological progress will allow us to utilize our leisure time better. Electronic devices in the field of communications can bring a new dimension to cultural events

[3] This will not be true, in general, for executives.

and popular entertainment. Technology and mass production will continue to expand our areas of choice.

Increasing urbanization, automation, and changes in the field of education—these are the three connected factors that lead us to the new instrument whose uses we are only just beginning to conceive: the computer. Computer technology and data systems will dominate the economy of 1980. We are discovering new possibilities and uses for them every day. Imagination, inspiration, intuition, and creative thought—which until now have belonged to the domain of the spirit—will now join forces with the electronic memory and the mathematical skills of the computer. This collaboration will stimulate new dimensions of thought and create a new kind of world.

Even before 1980 we will spend an increasing amount of time on improving our intellectual resources. This in turn will speed technological innovation and social change. But it will not be easy. One of the most serious problems of this new technological breakthrough is the widening gap between American industry and the rest of the world. This not only poses problems, but could lead to catastrophe.

We are in the process of *compressing time and space* in a way that was inconceivable ten years ago. Even more importantly, we are learning how to *intensify human experience* through centralized information and instant communication. This is a new world, one filled with adventure and risks.

CHAPTER 10

THE WORLD OF COMPUTERS

IN the White House there is an office of Science and Technology with a special assistant whose job is to study new techniques of communication and information involving computers. Until 1967 this job was held by William Knox, who for twenty years had been with Esso Research and Engineering Company. As Presidential adviser he gave an address on the future of the computer, from which extracts appear below.

For the first time since the invention of writing, man now stands on the threshold of being able to communicate—or to transfer information—while enjoying the best of these two means of communication—writing and talking. He will be able to use the vast store of information traditionally put into printed form, and will use it as easily and flexibly as he now talks to his neighbour. Modern technology will make this possible.

Until about 500 years ago, information was transferred from person to person either by talking or by hand-written manuscripts. There were few people who could spend time acquiring knowledge. The first revolutionary change was Gutenberg's invention of mechanical printing. The small store of information accumulated over thousands of years of human thought and activity was made accessible to more people. People also began to write more. Perhaps it was no coincidence that about 150 years after printing was invented and books were available through most of Western Europe, the scientific Renaissance was in full flower.

Two or three centuries later, the ever-intensifying search for better means of communication and the transfer of information led to the invention of the telegraph, telephone, phonograph, and camera. A few decades afterwards, the radio was invented. Technology had, in just half a century, added a number of new information transfer processes available for man's choosing, but, with the one exception of the motion picture, each new process transmitted either printed or spoken information, but not both. Until electronics.

Since then another technological revolution in information processes has occurred. It has had an enormous impact on modern society. But the gap between the industrialized and less-developed countries in information systems has been widened by the new technology. *It is now conceivable that we may no longer be able to communicate—simply communicate— with those who have not kept pace in their own technology with the scientific advancements we have incorporated into our own industrial structure and which are changing its very nature.*

The new information-processing revolution has coincided with an explosive growth in government-financed research and development. This has led to an equally rapid increase in published documents. Traditional documentation, typified by the scientific journal, proved unable to handle the increased volume of information, and a new documentary form, the technical report, came into being. About 100,000 such technical reports are published each year in the United States, in addition to about 900,000 articles in scientific and technical journals. Also, some 7,000 new books in this field are published every year—twice as many as ten years ago. This forces us to *rethink completely our methods for transferring information.*

We are now increasing our number of scientists and engineers by 10 per cent a year. Not only has the volume of new information increased dramatically, but equally dramatic is the speed with which American industry applies this information. It would have been, for example, almost impossible to have predicted that the jet aeroplane would replace the piston plane almost completely within ten years. This speed of change has far-reaching effects. Whereas a century ago there was time for reflection, time for the traditional information system to bring new information to the decision-makers before undesirable applications took place, the traditional information system is no longer adequate. If we continue to rely on them, we will be making our decisions more and more by chance.

The new revolution in information transfer will allow ideas to be used more effectively and more quickly. When computers were first developed several years ago, they were used for arithmetic and accounting. Now, however, we must think of them as instruments for transferring and dealing with every conceivable type of information. They can be used to process all the informational problems of industry, and decisions will be made on the basis of options provided by the computers. In 1955 there were 1,000 computers in the United States; by 1975 there will be 80,000. Today the federal government alone uses 2,000.

The great size of computers was once a problem, but by 1980 we will have machines a thousand times smaller, yet capable of doing the same work. Computer speeds will increase to a level of about one billion operations per second, and the cost per operation will be 200 times less than today.

Well before 1980, computers will be small, powerful, and inexpensive. Computing power will be available to anyone who needs it, or wants it, or can use it. In many cases the user will have a small personal console connected to a large, central computing facility where enormous electronic memories will store all aspects of knowledge. Corresponding developments in man-machine interaction will make it as easy to learn to use the new computers as to learn to drive a car.[1]

The more exciting developments in information processing are based on 'real-time' computer use. In these uses, the computer memory and processor are large enough to handle within seconds a variety of jobs, without needing to call for additional information from a non-computer store, such as punched cards. There is in these cases potential opportunity for the human operator to interact with the computer at a speed not too different from person-to-person conversation.

It is estimated that the entire store of information in the

[1] A French authority, Robert Lattès, director of the Société d'Information Appliquée (a branch of SEMA), says: 'Users will have to make a small effort, but not much more than they would to learn how to drive. And they won't fail any more often than they do their driver's test.'

world's libraries amounts to 10^{15} (one quadrillion, or one million billion) bits. This information is stored in the form of books and other printed documents, and is doubling every 15 to 20 years. A leading computer manufacturer has recently announced the commercial availability of a new type of direct-access computer memory that will hold 10^{12} bits (a thousand billion), or one-thousandth of the world's recorded information. There appears the possibility that by 1980 a small number of computers will replace *all the written documentation* existing in the world, and that they will work in 'real time'—replying to questions with information at the speed of human conversation.

Equally significant changes have been taking place in the technology of communication by satellites. Soon communications by satellites between continents, and even across the same continent, will be the fastest and cheapest means of communication. Further developments will see the transfer of images along with messages. Now limited because of expense, these developments will become commonplace by 1980.

Computer programmes are now becoming cheaper, faster, and more efficient. The latest development is called 'time-sharing', and allows the computer to answer questions from scores, or even hundreds, of users simultaneously. The time-shared computer system makes use of the time spent by a person between receipt of information and reaching a decision on his next step. This time, necessary to the human user, is wasted time to the computer. Clever instructions or programmes have been developed for the ultra-large, ultra-fast computers which switch the computer from one user to another in fractions of a second. These computers are like a telephone exchange with lines emanating from a single brain (in this case, the computer's central memory where facts are stored). Plans are being laid for systems serving 250 users simultaneously.

The development of the direct-access, time-shared computer system, with remote terminals, such as teletypewriters and dial telephones, is the revolutionary development of the future. The user will not need to write, or print, or even punch a keyboard; he need only speak to the computer, which will answer at the speed of a business conversation.

This conversation between the user and the computer can be by instantaneous typed messages, or by human voice over a conventional telephone. Such a system is in commercial use in the U.S., giving stock quotations in response to inquiries made by simply dialing the appropriate alphabetical symbols.

The examples cited above share an important characteristic: the human user has, in effect, coupled the computer's fantastic memory and calculating speed to his immediate requirements for information. This memory, as we have seen, can include an important part of all the printed documents in the libraries of the world. It is difficult to imagine the developments that will follow from these new techniques which change our methods for gathering information, and thus for performing work. But we do know that these developments will dramatically transform the industrial society in which we live.[2]

The federal government has already begun a series of programmes, in cooperation with large corporations, to determine the best uses for these new methods of gathering and diffusing information. A report has been made to the President recommending that the federal government should assume a responsibility to insure that there exists within the United States at least one copy of every significant document in the world-wide scientific and technical literature. The report also recommended the establishment of a top-level federal organization to guide and oversee the development of an integrated national network of document-handling systems in science and technology.

Some federal agencies have moved rapidly in the past three to five years to establish computer-based information services. Among these agencies are the Atomic Energy Commission, National Aeronautics and Space Administration, National Library of Medicine, the Department of Defense, and the Department of Commerce. Each of these agencies has giant computers working on 'real time', with individual consoles spread across the United States.

The increasing pressures on all learned professions and disciplines to apply existing knowledge will soon shatter the almost exclusive reliance of humanists and social scientists on the printed word. The computer will be the primary tool for

[2] Robert Lattès: 'Society, from an economic or industrial point of view, will be organized around information devices, for they augment man's cerebral capacities, while the first industrial revolution augmented only his muscular capacities.'

documentation, the storing of information, and the solving of day-to-day problems. By 1980 there will be a number of national electronic information centres. These 'computer utilities' will eventually be as cheap and as commonplace as electricity and water utilities.

Application of these new methods to education is lagging, but should develop spectacularly over the next decade. Part of the lag is due to the problem of cost. Schools and colleges are traditionally poor and unprepared to undertake new educational programmes that would utilize the full potential of computers. But over the next decade two new factors will reduce this problem: massive government assistance, and much cheaper costs for computer programming. By 1980, and probably before, most American schools and colleges will have consoles linked to giant computers dealing with every field of knowledge. Scheduling classes, and even pupils, will be routinely done by computer.

Perhaps the largest barrier to achieving the potential benefits of the new information-processing technologies will prove to be a lack of understanding about its possibilities. The changes in information transfer processes are too radical for the present generation in management to feel comfortable with them and to push for their adoption. But within the time span of this forecast, a new generation of management will have taken over, and rapid exploitation of the new technologies will take place.

The need for education and retraining in the new technologies is obvious. Change is likely to be so rapid that education in the classic sense of the term will be insufficient to our needs. We will be forced to readjust ourselves continually to change, and to organize educational retraining programmes for those who cannot interrupt their work life for more formal education. Many thousands of computer programmers and technical specialists will be required. Then, the computers themselves will teach and programme their own techniques. Before we reach that point— that is, *before 1980*—our political leaders will have to find answers to the social implications raised by the computer.

PART 3

EUROPE IN CONFUSION

STATE OF THE UNION

AFTER having examined the invasion of American industry in Europe, we then tried to go behind the lines of this operation. We should now keep two things in mind:

1. The American challenge is not basically industrial or financial. It is, above all, a challenge to *our intellectual creativity and our ability to turn ideas into practice.* We should have the courage to recognize that our political and mental constructs—our very culture—is being pushed back by this irresistible force.

2. America today still resembles Europe—with a 15-year head start. She belongs to the same industrial society. But in 1980 the United States will have entered another world, and if we fail to catch up, the *Americans will have a monopoly on know-how, science, and power.*

Forecasts indicate that two or three countries (Sweden and Japan, each in its own way) will stay on the same level with the United States by concentrating their efforts on special areas. But they will not be strong enough to deal with the U.S. as equals, nor will they be truly competitive. If Europe, like the Soviet Union, is forced out of the running, the United States will stand alone in its futuristic world. This would be unacceptable for Europe, dangerous for America, and disastrous for the world.

Variety of choice, checks and balances, and competition are vital elements of progress and freedom in each community. They are even more vital on the international level. If the United States had a monopoly on technological progress, it would lose the stimulation that comes from competition. There are already symptoms that this is happening.

75

All by themselves, without the help of comparisons and dialogues with others, the Americans would have the task of working out future forms of social organization. The struggle for progress, which holds as many dangers as opportunities, would be pursued without the restraining influence of an equal power, and the risks of error and distortion would multiply. A nation holding a monopoly of power would look on imperialism as a kind of duty, and would take its own success as proof that the rest of the world should follow its example. Thus it is no exaggeration to say that Europe holds more than her own destiny in her hands.

Ten years ago Europe showed that she understood the challenge of American power, and she did something about it by building such organizations as the Coal and Steel Community, Euratom, and the Common Market. Today the balance sheet is in: *Europe has created a market, but she has not transformed herself into a great power.* Even this market, as we have seen, does not help her so much as it does the American industrial machine.

Looking at the first ten years of the Common Market, the Compagnie Lambert concluded: 'One of the things we could have expected from the Common Market was the creation of large European corporations capable of meeting international, and particularly American, competition. The technological and financial gap separating the two continents should have been narrowed, Europe should have gained new strength in the areas of scientific research and technological innovation, and thereby been restored to economic and financial power. So far this has not happened. *The gap between the two continents has widened.*'

Raymond Aron reached a similar conclusion in 1966 regarding what he calls the failure of the Common Market: 'The failure of the Common Market is neither monetary nor commercial, but purely industrial. It can be summed up in a simple example: when a French or Italian firm gets into trouble, it usually turns for help to an American corporation rather than to another European firm. It is as though the effect of the Common Market was not to bring American capital to European industry, but to increase direct capital investments by American corporations.'

Since the resolution of the Common Market crisis, which erupted on June 30, 1965, public opinion assumes that Europe is once again moving ahead. This is true in certain secondary areas, but not in the critical areas which could allow us to escape American colonization. Here Europe is falling even further behind.

After the long paralysis of the Common Market following the June 1965 crisis, a number of important agreements were reached. One dealt with the common agricultural policy, and a settlement was reached on primarily financial grounds. Others related to a decision by the Six to eliminate all tariffs between the member countries on 1 July 1968. Most of the discussion at Brussels during the past few years has been on the customs union and the agricultural accord. The agreement reached is part of a global package deal by which France gained important agricultural advantages in exchange for her acceptance of a *free exchange policy* for industrial products, a policy particularly desired by Germany. This opens an enormous free trade zone and an industrial market of global scope to American industry and the dozen largest European firms. But where in all this is there any sign of European *power*?

The authors of the Treaty of Rome understood that before the total elimination of tariffs it would be necessary to make certain decisions on common economic policy by a simple majority rather than by unanimous vote. But this rule was set aside because of French objections during the crisis of June 1965. The result has been to water down the European Community and limit its ambitions.

There is little chance that by the time tariffs are fully eliminated, we will have breached a common policy on energy or scientific policy. On the matter of energy, several nations stick to the expensive mistakes of a so-called 'patriotic' policy devised by a French minister of industry. As for scientific policy, the Common Market Commission recently observed, in rather strong words for technocrats: 'If the six nations of the Community continue to remain the world's major importers of inventions and exporters of brains, as they have been for a generation, they will condemn themselves to an increasing underdevelopment that will soon be impossible to reverse.'

The solution to the scientific problem, which holds the key to the others, lies in the creation of a European technological community that the British have been trying to stimulate. 'A European technological community,' says *The Guardian*, 'is the real Europe of the future. To build it will be a test of nationalism versus rationalism... It will demand far-reaching psychological changes. But the only alternative is economic decline, and probably complete domination by the United States.'

In scientific matters the French maintain that the Common Market Commission may engage in 'studies', but that 'decisions' may be reached only by unanimous agreement among the member nations. For this reason Europe, so far as the institutions set up at Luxembourg and Brussels are concerned, is not becoming stronger, but weaker.

The oldest of the Common Market institutions is the Coal and Steel Community, dating from 1949. According to Paul Fabra of *Le Monde*: 'There is no longer a Common Market in coal because, in fact if not in law, there is no European capital in Luxembourg to direct the mining operations, and each government has gone back to managing its own affairs.'

The same thing applies to steel. 'Nothing happens in Luxembourg except crises,' says French foreign minister Couve de Murville. To which the coordinating office of the Common Market steelworkers' and miners' unions replied: 'The Coal and Steel Community is weak because it has been denied the power it is now criticized for not exercising.'

The Coal and Steel Community was created in a time of poverty, and the moment of truth was bound to come when that period was over. This has now happened. Faced with over-capacities that must be handled by group decisions, the member countries refuse to cooperate and instead play by their own rules. Germany's reply to France's long-term plan for the iron and steel industry, worked out between French businessmen and the minister of finance, was to form a new cartel of German firms. Belgium and Luxembourg took the same path. Each national steel group has fallen back on itself rather than co-operating with the others.

Euratom. The communal research programme that was supposed to allow the Europeans to pool their nuclear efforts and overcome their backwardness, has been virtually buried. Two distinguished Frenchmen, Louis Armand and Etienne

Hirsch, successive presidents of Euratom, have both had to resign after declaring that it was impossible to reconcile the aims of this organization with the national policies that the member nations, following France's example, have undertaken. One of the laboratory triumphs of the Euratom scientists was the development of a new kind of electrical reactor system called the 'Orgel'. But it took so long to get the six national governments to agree on how it should be produced that the Americans, who were several years behind in this field, will have their product on the market before the Europeans.

Euratom is condemned to failure by the theory of *fair return*. It is a term that should be understood by anyone interested in European economic policy and its future. According to this theory, each of the member states must receive as much in contracts and subsidies as it puts into Euratom. Every state, in other words, must get its share of the business. Delegates to the organization spend most of their time making sure their governments get a 'fair return' on what they put in. The logic of such a system is obviously contrary to industrial efficiency, for it works against central authority and internal dynamism in the organization—and thus undermines its *raison d'être*. This is the main reason for the failure of Euratom.

In Luxembourg, as in Brussels, we have entered a phase of 'communal polycentrism'. European centre of gravity is shifting away from communal institutions because the national governments are continually reinforcing their decision-making powers. It is not unfair to say that the European *community is falling apart*.

But, it can be said, these different communal institutions are only administrative organs. The essential thing is industry. How is European industry developing as it faces its American rival?

A great deal remains up in the air, since there has been no reply to the proposal of the Common Market Commission for a law governing European-scale corporations. France proposed a uniform corporate law, based upon an accord reached among the member states. The Common Market Commission said that introducing such a uniform law into the various national laws would still not solve the basic question of how to transfer the headquarters of a corporation from one country to another without going through lengthy formalities. The Commission then proposed a reasonable solution: the drafting of a body of European law. Such a law would create a situation of equality for both corporations and shareholders. In this way, mergers would not involve a change of nationality, but a Europeanization. 'This solution,' writes Pierre Drouin of *Le Monde*, 'is the most logical one, but there is no chance that it will be accepted at this time by France, since it is based upon the acceptance of supranationality.'

A comparison of European and American corporations during recent years shows that there are only a few firms in the Community with the scope and structure of American firms.[1] From this we can now draw a conclusion.

In a protected economy, of the kind we have had for the past century, neither a corporation's growth nor its financial structure was vitally important. The essential fact was that the national economy had to be capable of producing according to national needs. This was, above all, a question of technical equipment. Most investments involved merely the replacement of plant and equipment, and it mattered little whether or not the entrepreneur resorted to external methods of finance, such as loans. Still used to such an economy, we are a long way from putting sufficient emphasis on the financial structure of our corporations.

In a rapidly developing economy, on the other hand—one marked by technological progress and tough competition—the value of a corporation and its ability to fight back depend less on its factories and machinery than on non-material factors such as its profit and loss, its creativity, and its sales organization. This is true to such a degree that many firms in Europe today are drowning from overinvestment.

A considerable number of European corporations, despite their currently favourable circumstances, of trying to assure themselves a future worthy of their own past, have virtually given up the effort. These firms, some of which are very large, are structurally too weak to finance, from their own funds, investments necessary to achieve the kind of growth enjoyed by their American competitors. This weakness has only a minor effect on their sales in the short run, but endangers their growth and their chances of survival.

[1] *See* Chapter 6, 'The Growth Spiral'.

There are only three possible strategies for European industry today. We have still not made a conscious choice among them.

1. Continue along the same path and face a double decline in our business level and our financial structure. For a time our industry could continue its struggle with American competition, but this would only delay the day of reckoning. Financial erosion would continue until European industrialists realized that the lesser evil lay in selling their businesses to an American competitor for two or three times the value of their capitalization—which is the going rate today. This is a strategy of retreat which leads to industrial annexation.

2. A cleverer strategy for the firm would be to play a complementary role in the American economy by specializing in those areas where Europe still has an advantage—largely because of lower labour costs and the use of foreign patents. While this is good strategy for a single firm, if it were applied throughout Europe it would mean splitting the world economy into three zones: a first zone of highly developed technological societies responsible for discoveries and innovations; a second zone, mainly Europe, whose role would be to produce the discoveries made elsewhere; finally, a third zone of underdeveloped nations to provide raw materials and simple industrial products using traditional methods. This division of labour is now taking place. The nations of Europe would become *industrial satellites* and could not hope to play a major role on the world stage. The more rigorous the control exercised by the dominant power, the less chance there would be for economic growth in Europe.

3. As an alternative to annexation or satellization, there is the choice of *competition*. This demands that European businesses, particularly those in the area of 'Big Science', become fully competitive on the global market. Figures show that they cannot do this from their own resources, and that government assistance is necessary, particularly in such areas as electronics, data processing, space research, and atomic energy.

How should such massive government aid for the construction of giant European industries be carried out? On a national level, given the relative weakness of the individual states, such a solution would demand strict specialization. Each state would have to opt for the Swedish or Swiss example, specializing in two or three industrial areas and concentrating its resources along these lines.[2]

Only at a European, rather than a national, level could we hope to meet the American challenge on all major fronts. But not just any kind of European cooperation. We will see why what we call international 'cooperation' in industry is only an empty slogan. If we want to achieve our ambitions, make unpopular decisions, avoid duplication and waste, and draw ourselves up to a level where we can compete, we will have to give the Common Market financial power of its own.

Leaving aside questions of ideology, there is no other solution to our industrial problems than forming some kind of federal organization, one whose outlines we shall try to draw as precisely as possible so that we can avoid the emotions and polemics that go with abstract ideas.

For the moment Europe refuses to make this choice, preferring various formulas for cooperation between governments. The limitations inherent in this kind of venture merit closer investigation.

[2] The Swedish model is rich in social potential, but Sweden has no ambitions to be a world power.

CHAPTER 12

THE CONCORDE AFFAIR

AMONG the attempts at economic cooperation, the most successful has been the supersonic 'Concorde' airliner being built by Britain and France. This project offers an interesting comparison between limited international cooperation and a real joint effort of the kind that would involve long-term scientific planning and centralized control at the industrial level.

The Concorde project seemed to offer the best possible conditions for a successful collaboration: there were only two partners, both had political reasons for wanting to make the effort work, the airline industries in both countries were faced with similar problems, the partners had about the same strength in population, financial structure, and technology. But we have learned the hard way just how inadequate this kind of collaboration can be.

At the end of 1964 the Labour government under Harold Wilson decided to abandon Concorde as part of its austerity programme. This naturally provoked a violent reaction in Paris —indeed, such a reaction that the British had to reverse gears and resume the programme. The Wilson government, however, was simply observing the rule of De Gaulle's famous *Europe des patries*—a Europe of nations.

Later General Puget, head of the French side of the Concorde project and one of its original promoters, was fired without warning (either to himself or to the British), and was replaced by a police commissioner who had just turned down an ambassadorship. This in turn provoked a *crise de confiance* in Britain, just as the earlier British decision had provoked a similar crisis of confidence in France.

83

At each step of the way it was obvious that this was a shaky operation. It would be hard to imagine any major corporation tolerating a project that involved such fits and starts. But eventually necessity triumphed over these obstacles. Work proceeded on the Concorde, and there is now a good chance that the project will actually come off. This is a very important and very expensive industrial effort. Tomorrow's aviation is clearly going to be supersonic, and to give the Americans a monopoly is to let them take over the skies. In principle the Concorde project will succeed. But succeed in doing what?

During the switch-over from propeller planes to jets, Europe was outpaced by America and fell out of the race. She will win the second lap by producing the first faster-than-sound intercontinental commercial plan. The Concorde test flights are scheduled for 1968, when André Turcat, chief pilot of Sud-Aviation, will take the plane in the air for twenty minutes over Toulouse. First full-scale deliveries are scheduled for 1971, while the American entry, the Boeing SST, will not be ready until two or three years later—probably in 1974.

But the performance of the two planes will be different. The Concorde will fly at Mach 2·2 (that is, 2·2 times the speed of sound), while the Boeing will fly at Mach 2·7. The Concorde will carry only 136 passengers, while the Boeing will carry 300. Clearly the Boeing is technically superior, but since the Anglo-French project has a three-year head start, it has a good chance of becoming commercially profitable during its lead time.[1] Paris and London explain the Boeing's technical superiority by pointing out that the decision to build the Concorde was made in 1962, while the Americans did not enter the race until 1967. Naturally their plane would be more technologically advanced. This explanation should be looked into more closely, for it involves an analysis and a prediction that go to the root of the problem.

The American plane will not be simply a more advanced version of its European rival, reflecting a difference of a few

[1] Even this is uncertain. By the summer of 1967 the airlines had ordered 74 Concordes (250 sales are needed to break even), as against 112 options for the Boeing SST, including those of Air France.

years between the models. It represents a radical advance in aviation technology. The Americans did not begin their plans in 1967 or in 1962, but in 1950. The sad truth is that the Concorde, attractive and daring in design though it may be, is the *last of the classic planes*, while the Boeing is the first of a new generation of planes developed exclusively for supersonic flight. The Concorde will have a career of a few brief years, while the Boeing, based on ideas which are revolutionary in the context of today's planes, will have a 15- to 20-year career, like its jet-propelled predecessors.

The difference of speed is crucial. Between Mach 2·2 and Mach 2·7 there is a barrier, similar to the sound barrier, that is known as the 'heat barrier'. At Mach 2·2 air resistance will heat the Concorde's 'skin' to 150 degrees Centigrade (300°F), while at Mach 2·7 the surface temperature of the Boeing will hit 270 degrees. At 150 degrees it is still possible to use classic metal alloys; at 270 degrees entirely new alloys are necessary.

The problem is acute because this is a passenger-carrying plane. Such temperatures, and even higher ones, are common for ballistic missiles, but only for short periods. Since a missile flies only once, classic alloys can be used. The supersonic plane, on the other hand, will be subject to tremendous heat for some two hours, and the airlines which buy these planes want them to last for at least 30,000 hours of flying time. During these 30,000 hours the plane's surface must not suffer from metal fatigue or distortion.

The Concorde will be built from a classic aluminium alloy that has been used for several years and satisfies the specifications of the airlines. At Mach 2·7, however, only stainless steel and titanium can resist the heat, but since stainless steel is too heavy, only titanium has a future in supersonic aviation. The Boeing naturally will be built of titanium. This will allow it eventually to improve its performance, to exceed its predicted speed and go beyond Mach 3, and to have a longer profitable life-span. The Concorde, shut out by the heat barrier, has no future.

The second basic difference between these two planes is the choice of a 'swing-wing' design by Boeing. The pilot can push forward and retract the plane's wings as the driver of a car shifts gears. Lockheed, which competed with Boeing for the government contract to produce the supersonic plane, chose a fixed wing like that of the Concorde, and lost out.

The advantages of the swing-wing are crucial. They allow a plane flying at three times the speed of sound to slow down far below the speed of sound by pushing forward its wings. Thanks to the swing-wing design, the Boeing, despite its enormous weight and a speed that will exceed Mach 3, will be able to use existing runways. American supersonic aviation is based on the commercial imperative of never demanding completely new ground facilities and continuing to use existing airports. The advantage is obvious.

Because of the growing traffic at international airports, a plane often has to circle the ground while waiting for permission to land. These landing delays will be difficult for fixed-wing supersonic planes, and they will need special landing facilities. The Boeing, however, by stretching forward its wings, can adjust more easily to normal air traffic.

Finally, there is the serious problem of sonic boom, now under study everywhere. It could lead to the prohibition of supersonic flights over populated areas. Such a ban would threaten all the supersonic planes, but the Boeing could adapt by flying at supersonic speeds over oceans and sparsely inhabited areas, and at subsonic speeds over populated areas.

On the two essential points—use of an entirely new metal to crack the heat barrier, and the swing-wing to change speed— the technological and commercial superiority of the American plane, a superiority of conception, is so dramatic that we have to ask why the Europeans never came to grips with it. We could have mastered both of these problems. It was a question of vision, planning, decision-making, and risk-taking. In short, of organization.[2] Here is the proof.

Titanium was discovered simultaneously by a British clergyman and an Austrian scientist at the beginning of the last century. It is not a rare metal like copper or tin, but is among

---

[2] Concorde supporters argue, with some justice, that it was primarily a question of price: the Boeing costs two or three times as much and thus was too expensive. This is a weak argument, since price is never a reason in itself, but can only be judged in relation to the product. The Boeing will be cheaper per passenger-seat than the Concorde.

the world's nine most common elements. Deposits are particularly abundant in Canada and Australia, and thus easily available to the British.

The swing-wing was developed before the war, and the first prototype was flown by the German firm, Messerschmitt, near the end of hostilities. In essence, the wing is basically a pivot with hydraulic jacks near the centre. This idea was developed in Europe. Since the Europeans had titanium and knew about the swing-wing, why did nothing ever come of it?

What is involved here is the very process of research and development that lies at the heart of modern industry. This is what separates a theory from its industrial application—the organization of intellectual and scientific potential for a concentrated effort.

The American project began when the U.S. government agency that was later to become the National Aeronautics and Space Administration (NASA) contracted with private industry for a supersonic plane, the Bell X5, using some of the German plans. Test flights took place in 1951. The first operational swing-wing plane was the F-111, built by General Dynamics, with prototypes flown in 1964 and 1965. Two of these planes crashed—the first because of a jammed pivot, the second because swing-wing design had not yet overcome the aerodynamic problems of low-altitude flight. Twenty-three more planes were put into production. By this time the U.S. government had spent $2 billion, through federal contracts, for swing-wing prototypes.

Then Boeing took over, devoted a million hours of study to the project and 10,000 hours in wind-tunnel tests to improve performance. This took not only a great deal of time, but concentrated effort and decisive management. Boeing engineers calculated that the supersonic commercial plane should be able to endure temperatures ranging from −50 degrees (−172°F) to +270 degrees Centigrade (+518°F). To do this they had to form metal alloys at minus 200 degrees Centigrade so that there would be no deformation at any temperature. Test conditions were set up to reproduce real flight temperatures and subject the swing-wing pivot to pressures of 2,000 tons (actual flight pressure would be close to 1,500 tons).

Apart from its financial cost, a job of this scope demands

such technical coordination and such a long time for completion
that European technicians working on the Concorde project
did not feel able to take it on within the organizational limits
imposed upon them. The French engineers of Sud-Aviation put
it frankly: 'If they had told us to build a swing-wing plane, we
could have done it. But we would have been scared to death all
the time we were doing it. To be honest, we did everything we
could to avoid it.'[3]

A not unreasonable attitude, considering the restrictions and
the constant stops and starts involved. Not unreasonable, either,
considering that in July 1967 a much simpler Anglo-French
scheme to build a swing-wing military plane was cancelled
without warning by French defence minister Pierre Messmer.
The order was passed on to his British colleague, Denis Healey,
who had no choice but to accept it in his 5 July speech to the
House of Commons. This French move was politically inspired,
for it forced the British to substitute American F-111's for the
cancelled plane. This, coming at the very moment when Britain
was seeking entry into the Common Market, was used to furnish
another 'proof' of her dependence on the United States.

The titanium story is equally instructive. For many years
titanium was a chemical curiosity. Although it could be combined with virtually every known substance, it seemed to have
little practical application. At melting temperature it shows a
disastrous affinity for oxygen, nitrogen, and hydrogen—in other
words, for air and water. But when adulterated by these elements, it loses its original properties. This posed a difficult,
almost unique, problem.

Serious attempts to make titanium usable were begun after
the Second World War. The decision, in this case as well, was
made by the U.S. government through the Bureau of Mines,
working in conjunction with the Department of Commerce.
First the metal was turned into a gas, titanium tetrachloride, by
heating it to 800 degrees Centigrade. In this gaseous state its
temperature was reduced by 900 degrees and molten magnesium
added. This turned it into a kind of 'sponge', which was then
crushed and cleaned of impurities in an acid bath. Finally, still

[3] A further proof that it was possible: Marcel Dassault, head of
Sud-Aviation, has since developed a swing-wing military prototype
without outside assistance.

in an absolute vacuum, the metal was cast into ingots by electric arc. The containers themselves were made of titanium, since no other metal was strong enough. The quality of the refined titanium depends on the purity of each of the substances used in the different operations. In titanium metallurgy, as with the various 'atomic' metals, there was a *qualitative* industrial advance and the development of a totally new technology.

Great efforts were required to develop a metallurgical process to deal with titanium, and the task is still not completed. Welding of heavy-gauge titanium sheets poses problems which so far have prevented the construction of pure titanium nuclear submarines. If this project had not been underwritten by the federal government through research grants, tax write-offs, purchase contracts, and even investment loans, it would have been interrupted a dozen times.

Because of difficulties encountered in research, consumption of titanium dropped from 11,000 tons in 1956 to 4,000 tons in 1959. The U.S. even had to cancel production of new bombers. It seemed that the whole titanium project was a failure. But at government insistence work continued, and in 1965 success was finally achieved. Not only was the process perfected, but, as is common in the industry, the price of the metal began to go down. Once the links were worked out, money could be saved on waste, tests, and production methods. Thus sponge titanium, which cost $5 a pound in 1953, today costs American firms only $1·25. As a result, the Boeing SST, which seemed hopelessly expensive during the initial development of titanium, will now cost little more than if classic metals were used.

A new stage of technology has been reached. It took years of work in the laboratory, years of determination by the directors of the project, massive federal aid, and extensive planning and collaboration between the universities, the federal government, and the aviation industry. Now firms such as U.S. Steel invest heavily in titanium—not only for the Boeing SST, but for a gamut of other projects using advanced technology—just as they formerly invested in steel. A new field of industry has been opened up.

The swing-wing plane and the development of titanium sum up the problem. Contrary to what the British and French directors of the Concorde project may say, American superiority is not basically a question of dollars but of industrial structure, farsighted vision, and centralized control.

The engineers at Sud-Aviation explain, with some justice: 'If the United States is so far ahead, it is because the Americans had so much at their disposal after the war that they could experiment in different fields without worrying about the risks involved.' This is true. With limited means it is not possible to do much more than fill immediate needs. Yet *future profits depend on long-term planning*. With insufficient means and a structural incapacity to take major risks, we limit the potential of our own future.

It is worth noting that the Russians, who are far from enjoying a Western European standard of living, but who realize the importance of long-term planning, have just built a titanium conversion plant to cover a wide range of future needs. Like the Americans, they are mobilizing public opinion in support of their scientific and industrial projects. At the last Air Show in Paris, the hammer and sickle that crowned the Soviet pavilion was made of titanium.

This is the story of the Concorde. Rather than reiterating its lesson, we will pass on to another experiment in European industrial cooperation—the conquest of space.

CHAPTER 13

THE SPACE ADVENTURE

THREE HUNDRED European firms, representing more than two million wage earners, have formed a group to push the European governments into the space race. The conquest of space has a great industrial impact on any nation or group of nations making the race. It requires technical skills far superior to those we now have, and thus it serves as an incentive to progress. Because of the 'fall-out' from space research, American industry has been able to make important technological breakthroughs in refractory metals, computers, and equipment for working in vacuums. Within a few years new methods of communication will be relayed through space. Already channels for intercontinental telecommunication via satellite are being assigned. The only existing company in this field is American.

According to the manifesto of industrialists belonging to the organization known as EUROSPACE: 'The total space budgets of all Western European countries combined, including government programmes and contributions to various organizations, is less than one-thirtieth of NASA's budget. Unless Europe makes a determined effort to catch up, commercial satellites of the type now becoming operational—telecommunications, television, meteorology, and navigation—will pass under American control for many years.

'While the nations of Europe might conceivably decide not to compete in a particular branch of an industry, how can they legitimately stay out of an entire area? Particularly when this is an area with enormous development potential and one where the United States has made advancements exceeding all expectations? A European abdication in an area of such importance

91

would not only be an economic fact but a historic fact that would mark the beginning of her own self-willed decline.

'Billions of dollars in NASA funds started flowing into American industry more than two years ago. By 1970 a wave of American-built space equipment will inundate much of the world. We have to recognize that, aside from certain scientific experiments, no single European nation can carry on a major space programme. Joint action is essential. There is an international organization for satellite communication that will soon include navigation and meteorology. Global competition is the rule. Unless the nations of Europe succumb to bilateralism and try to work out separate deals with the United States—thereby losing much of their identity—they will have to join together for space research.

'A joint effort would include all areas of space technology. The financial effort needed to carry out such an effort will be made only if there is *total coordination to eliminate oversights and duplication.* This is what NASA does in the United States.'

What EUROSPACE wants, in other words, is to create a European NASA. Nonetheless, Europe has not remained completely on the sidelines during the spectacular space race between the Russians and the Americans. Since this is the greatest industrial adventure of our time, the one that has the most meaning for the younger generation, it is important to look at the positive as well as the negative side of Europe's efforts.

Europeans initially wasted a good deal of time by indecision. Long after the launching of the first space satellite (Sputnik, on 4 October 1957) they kept asking how they could possibly take part in the space race. No European country could hope to make much of an impact acting by itself, but Europeans could not agree on a joint effort—partly for political reasons, and partly because they were reluctant to reveal military secrets.

Things began to change almost by accident in 1961. The British took the initiative, although their plan could hardly be called visionary, since it involved little more than trying to find a commercial use for a British missile, the 'Blue Streak', that could no longer be used by the military. It seemed that this outmoded missile could serve as a first-stage launcher for commercial satellites. After putting out a few feelers on the Continent, the British asked France to join with them in offering a satellite-launching missile programme to the other Common Market countries.

The British and the French reached agreement in principle, and a proposal was presented to the interested European countries in Strasbourg in February 1961. A year later, in April 1962, seven nations signed an accord setting up the European Launcher Development Organization: ELDO.[1]

The countries involved in developing the launcher did not devote enough time and effort to preparing the programme. Each country worked separately on the scientific and technical problems of the operation, with almost no contact between officials at the international level. When political negotiations began, countries lined up in blocs against one another, making it impossible to discuss the project in detail. This required various political compromises. However desirable the objectives may have appeared, they could not be reached because of disagreements on a number of issues. Delays piled up, and the accord did not become effective until March 1964—two years after it had been signed.

It stated: 'The objective of ELDO is the development and construction of space-launching devices and the equipment necessary for their practical utilization.' The programme called for the construction of the ELDO-A missile, to be built in the following stages:

First stage: the British 'Blue Streak' rocket (manufactured by Hawker Siddeley and Rolls Royce).

Second stage: the French rocket 'Coralie' (developed by the Laboratoire de Recherches Balistiques et Aerodynamiques).

Third stage: a German rocket (developed and built by Entwicklungsring-Nord).

The first series of experimental satellites would be built in Italy, the ground stations in Belgium, and the long-range guiding equipment and ground apparatus in Holland. ELDO-A was supposed to put an 800-kilogram satellite into orbit 550 kilometres above the earth. But from the beginning there were problems:

[1] The seven member countries of ELDO are: Germany, France, Britain, Italy, Belgium, Holland, and Australia.

1. The participating countries had never made a joint study of the whole system. Incredibly, the launching device—that is, the missile—had been agreed upon without any of the participating countries knowing what they were going to launch. There had been no discussions with ESRO,[2] which was making a study of satellites that might be put into orbit.

2. The international secretariat had no real authority, no competent technical staff, and no direct influence on the development of the programme. It could not correct the inadequacies of the original agreement or pinpoint, through systematized and centralized analysis, serious miscalculations in the anticipated budgets.

3. Finally, and most importantly, since the financial share of various parts of the programme had been worked out before the development contracts were signed, each of the participants immediately incorporated their assignments into their own national programmes. The international character of the project was compromised, since each country was using its contribution to finance the part of the programme it was conducting, and even to pay for purely national projects that were not part of the programme.

The British, for example, soon perfected their 'Blue Streak' missile and used the rest of their budget to develop control equipment that was not included in the ELDO programme. The Germans devoted their ELDO contribution to developing ground-testing facilities which would eventually be useful in setting up their own space programme. There are similar examples for all the members of ELDO. Each country used the project to finance its own national space programme, since the organizers gave no exact directions, and the international secretariat exercised no direct control. It is hardly surprising that an organization so badly conceived went through two grave crises within three years.

New estimates drawn up by the ELDO secretariat in 1964 showed that the programme could not be finished within the predicted time, and the launching, scheduled for 1965, was delayed until 1968. The cost of the programme had also

[2] ESRO (European Space Research Organization) coordinates the construction of satellites. Its members are the seven ELDO countries, plus Spain, Denmark, Sweden, and Switzerland.

doubled, with the budget rising from $196 million to $404 million. It was these problems, these results, and these mistakes that triggered the 'French crisis' of 1965.

Faced with rising costs and further delays, the French government threatened to withdraw from the ELDO-A project. Paris pointed out that this expensive European missile could be used only by ESRO, an organization no one had ever bothered contacting. The whole operation seemed unprofitable and illogical.[3] The French attitude was understandable, and was based on more than a desire for industrial efficiency. Having financial troubles of their own at the time, the French preferred to devote their resources to their limited, but independent and very expensive, military programme.

After long and thorny discussions, the French changed their minds and proposed an alternative: abandon ELDO-A and instead build a more expensive, but more useful missile, ELDO-B. This missile would use 'Blue Streak' in the first stage and combine it with liquid hydrogen and oxygen, which would give it the power to put into orbit a satellite with more than twice the payload of ELDO-A, thereby making it possible to launch meteorological and telecommunications satellites. Although it involved higher costs and further delays, such a programme was within Europe's means. Was the French government being sincere, or was it providing itself with an excuse for a tactical retreat? We will never know, since France's partners all turned down the project.

Finally, after more political delays, the member states agreed in the spring of 1965 to pursue the original ELDO-A project and to double its budget. But they were unable to agree on a reform of the secretariat. Less than a year later, in 1966, a new dispute broke out: the 'British crisis'.

Plagued by financial troubles and preferring to use their resources for their own programmes, the British had second thoughts about participating in certain technological aspects of the project. In the spring of 1966 they sent their ELDO

[3] By the summer of 1967 the use of the ELDO rocket by ESRO had still not been resolved' ESRO did not know whether or not the kind of satellites it was developing could be launched by ELDO-A, and reserved the right to choose American rockets to launch its satellites if their price and specifications were better.

associates a message questioning the very purpose of the programme and their own participation in it. This message contained more or less the same arguments the French had used, and that the British had earlier rejected.

But the other ELDO members stood firm, and the British withdrew their threats. In return, however, they demanded new studies of the programme, a management shake-up, and a revision of financial contributions. After heated discussions, ELDO's mission was reconfirmed with a new organizational setup and the following objectives:

1. The initial programme would be reoriented, with ELDO-A being given additional stages allowing it to put a 150-kilo satellite into a synchronous earth orbit (for telecommunications) in 1970–1971. Its name: ELDO-ASP.

2. Other changes involved the guidance system, the use of a ground station in Guyana, and development of long-life stabilization rockets for the satellites.

3. The budget was set at $626 million until 1971.

4. The secretariat was authorized to negotiate contracts with various national bodies, thereby gaining some international authority, and would be assisted by its own industrial team.

These decisions indicate that the European governments finally understand the importance of the project and the need for a radical change in its methods. But this is only a first step. ELDO reforms were adopted without resolving the other problems of European space research, particularly relations with ESRO—all this, ten years after the launching of Sputnik, six years after the first Anglo-French agreement, five years after the treaty of 'cooperation' among the European nations. As a result, even if ELDO-ASP is launched in 1971, it will put only a 150-kilo satellite into a synchronous 'stationary' orbit, while in 1967 the United States had half a dozen operational rockets capable of putting a two-ton payload into a synchronous orbit.

Considering such problems and crises, it might seem that nostalgic nationalism might give way to a greater sense of European realism—one that is finally being shown in some circles. Yet it remains to be seen whether government officials will listen to the warnings of scientists and businessmen. Our task will not be easy, and the Americans, despite appearances, won't simplify matters. They recently announced that they would turn over their 'Scout' missile free to any country wanting to launch scientific satellites. This is the rocket France used in launching her first satellite, the FR-1. The Russians are following the same tack, and Professor Sedov came to Paris with an important delegation to propose bilateral cooperation with France in all areas of space research. In order to save money, the French have agreed in principle to let the Russians launch a French satellite in 1971.

During all this manœuvring by the French, the British decided to build their own satellite-launcher, 'Black Arrow', which by 1969 is supposed to put British satellites into orbit from the base at Woomera in Australia—with American assistance. The Germans have not been twiddling their thumbs during this underground competition with ELDO, and have done their best to win American help. The U.S. recently incorporated them into their space programme by asking the Germans to build special equipment for probes of Jupiter.

In this area, more than anywhere else—since many industries depend on the space programme—the power rivalry is being carried on in full force. Neither America nor Russia wants Europe to become a real power in space. They are helped by the nationalism of European countries that prefer 'cooperation', even if it is only a synonym for impotence, to giving up their sovereignty in favour of European integration.

Space vehicles and satellites use titanium, beryllium, zirconium, and tantalus, metals that Europe is unfamiliar with and will never be able to develop if she gives up the space race. Launchers and missiles demand new techniques such as magnetic hammering, powder metallurgy, 'honeycomb' metal structures, and, of course, the calculating powers of integrated computers—all fields in which Europe is still in the testing stage, and in which progress depends, in large part, on the incentive of space. This gives only an idea of the advantages for industry and research if we created a European NASA—and of the dangers of dropping out of the space race.

Space research today is primarily 'chemical'. The Europeans still have the time, using their knowledge and their existing laboratories, to master this challenge. But time is running short, for the second space decade will see the advent of 'atomic' astronauts. Nuclear engines will be used to put giant satellites into orbit and to feed high-power transmitters. These future satellites and transmitters will make possible the direct transmission of television images through space, and 'real-time' long-distance conversation between computers on all points of the globe, as outlined in chapter 10. Once the machinery for mastering chemical astronautics has been set up, Europe should immediately plunge into atomic astronautics, which will be the basis for planetary exploration within another ten years.

On July 10 and 11, 1967, European ministers for scientific research met in Rome for a 'space conference'. At the conference there was a clash between the French and Italian delegates. The Italian minister, Leopoldo Rubinacci, said that Europe should not duplicate work being carried out by the Americans and the Russians—a dangerously equivocal position. The French delegate, for his part, declared that 'the absence of a long-term European space programme makes it impossible to define a short-term programme either in research or technology.' While this makes sense, it could also serve as an excuse for France to pursue her own military space programme. A few more 'space conferences' like this, and the Europeans will have little choice but to accept American offers to become subcontractors.

CHAPTER 14

BATTLE OF THE COMPUTERS

THE war is industrial, and its major battle is over computers. This battle is very much in doubt, but it has not yet been lost.

'Between 1970 and 1980', according to Jacques Maisonrouge,[1] 'the most important industry in the world, after oil and automobiles, will be computers.' This accords with the predictions of John Diebold, head of an international management consultant firm, who states: 'By 1970 computers will be the biggest single investment expense for a corporation, comprising at least 10 per cent of its total investment.' In 1968 the OECD (Organization for European Cooperation and Development) will publish a long comparative study based on research into the technological gap between Europe and America. Its conclusions, already released to European officials, are: 'Europe's technological lag is greatest in the field of computers, and is so severe that backwardness in other areas seems of minor importance. In fact, we have almost reached the point of no return in computer technology.'

The results of this study should be no surprise. For the past two years governments of Europe have known that they could neglect space for the time being, and continue to make less aeronautically-advanced planes than the Americans, but that they could not afford to let the U.S. control the world computer industry. And they have no excuse for doing so. The computer, the key to man's future, was conceived in Europe. Its conquest is less a matter of money than of being able to concentrate our intellectual resources, our talents of organization, and our

[1] Mr. Maisonrouge, 43 years old, is the French president of IBM-Europe. More about him later.

99

creativity. What we do with computers will tell us whether Europe can survive.

The first computer was put into operation in Berlin in 1941 by Konrad Zuse. The Z3, then the Z4, were electro-mechanical machines comparable to those developed by IBM at Harvard University in 1944. The Z3 was even faster, since its basic operation took only ·43 seconds, while the IBM machine took 5 seconds.

The first entirely electronic American machine, developed in 1946, required 18,000 tubes, as compared to 1,500 for the Zuse. Next to Germany, the most advanced country in computers was not the United States, but Britain. Moreover, until now, the computer industry has depended primarily on brain power and labour. Capital investment per employee is among the lowest for any industry. In this area the wealth of the United States has not been a great advantage.

While Americans are forward-looking in other areas, they took a long time to understand the role the computer would play in industrial development. In 1950, John Mauchly, father of the American computer industry, said that 'only four or five giant firms will be able to employ these machines usefully.' In 1960 U.S. government officials predicted that within five years 15,000 computers would be used in industry. By that date there were already 25,000 in use, and 40,000 today.

The Americans started late, made mistakes in their forecasts, were initially outpaced, and still have not solved all their problems. But they are surging ahead, and we have little time to catch up. Every new generation of computers—America is now starting on the third—represents a decisive technological advance, in fact a mutation, over the preceding one.

A decade ago, the first generation of computers was based on ordinary electronic equipment (tubes), and the machines themselves were relatively slow. The second generation, about five years ago, took a giant step forward by replacing the tubes with small transistors. The third generation, now being launched on an extraordinary gamble by IBM, uses the marvellously ingenious device of integrated circuits.

An integrated circuit is an electronic circuit which replaces a whole series of linked parts, such as tubes, transistors, condensors, resistors, etc. Newly-developed micro-circuits are able to replace, in a single square centimetre of plastic, eleven formerly interconnected pieces. Its advantages are formidable: simplicity, strength, size, and weight. Without integrated circuits there could be no giant space rockets capable of carrying tons of equipment on interplanetary trips. These integrated circuits have made such a difference that within a few years they are likely to replace all the electronic equipment we now use.

Integrated circuits are already being used on submarine-based Polaris missiles and on the swing-wing F-111 fighter. All the electronic equipment on the Boeing SST, and on the Concorde as well, will work from American-made integrated circuits. Today these circuits are made by three American firms—Fairchild, Texas Instruments, and Motorola.

The progress represented by the development of integrated circuits has been paid for by a highly-complicated technology and massive investments. OECD officials estimate that a firm manufacturing integrated circuits can amortize its research and make a profit only if it sells a million components a year. The entire European market can currently absorb only 250,000 components. Only if European industry were unified into a single community and plugged into an expanding European market could it hope to make integrated-circuit production profitable during the decade from 1970 to 1980. But so far every nation has been acting for itself, developing its own technology of integrated circuits, and wanting to have its own production centre—even though it is doomed to failure before it ever goes into operation. For this type of industrial investment a minimum market is essential, and European technicians are only now beginning to realize it.

Every European industrialist in the electronics field analyses IBM's experience in launching the third generation of computers, the famous series 360. Over a four-year period IBM invested $5 billion in this project—a sum equal to the total annual space budget of the U.S. government. To build the 360, IBM turned its administrative and management structure inside out. Executives who lost the company two years by ignoring the industrial possibilities of integrated circuits were replaced. With a new set of managers, IBM offered fantastic salaries to steal the best technicians it could find from its competitors. Even then it pulled off the gamble only thanks to its world-wide commercial network. It was because General Electric hoped to rival this network that it bought out Olivetti in Italy and Bull in France. What interested GE were the sales and maintenance outlets of these European firms, not their relatively weak technological potential.

If Europe is not to be defeated in this battle of computer manufacturing, it must immediately unify its efforts under a single command. While this battle is being fought, we are faced with the even more sophisticated battle of 'human input', which involves ways of organizing the use of computers and getting better performances out of them. This is what is called 'software'—hardware, of course, being the machine itself.

Software is a matter of application and research. The computer works entirely by means of binary electronic impulses performing high-speed operations. The problem is to develop languages by which man can communicate with the machine, and in which each word constitutes a specific part of the programme. Then technicians want to build a machine which, instead of using a keyboard and a mathematical language, will be able to read directly from printed texts or even manuscripts, and, as we have seen, be plugged in to the human voice.

IBM is now working on a machine which, instead of replying in a language of numbers which must be decoded, will project on a television screen a diagram which corresponds to the numbers. The engineer in charge can then correct the diagram with a single light-pen, and the machine will re-translate the diagram into numbers. This too is software.

'The development of information techniques,' says Robert Lattès, 'is basically a question of software, that is, of intelligence, for it involves purely cerebral creations which project the ingenuity and intelligence of man into the computer.'

A programmer named Mr. Rigal gives this example. Suppose we are dealing with partial differential equations. The computer, which can handle only arithmetic, and not analytic geometry, cannot solve the problem. In this case the question must be rephrased: a mathematician must substitute a linear, finite system for a non-linear, infinite system with partial differentials. Several solutions are possible. The choice of the best possible solution will depend on time and the operational perfection of the machine. This is a question of software.

From the moment the computer becomes an organ of information and management, and not merely a calculating machine, everything depends on how intelligently it is programmed, much more than on the technical perfection of the machine. The future of the computer belongs to experts in software, that is, to the best brains, rather than to the technicians who are experts in hardware. The problem, then, is a matter of research and coordinated teamwork.

Those who will not make the effort to win this battle will be dominated by those who learn to master computer technology. And in this field the losers will find that the purchase of industrial processes through patents and licenses runs at least 15 per cent higher than in other areas. In no other industry is colonization from abroad so oppressive. Yet, according to John Diebold, 'the real reign of the computer has only just begun. As an instrument of analysis, management, and decision-making, the computer will dominate industry by 1970.'

In order not to be outpaced by their competitors, American firms are investing in computer technology to the full limit of their means. Yet so intense is the rate of change and innovation that during a decade of production only one or two firms, out of nine or ten, have consistently been able to make a profit on their operations.

We can make an interesting comparison with Philips, the one European firm that had a real chance of competing with the Americans. But after estimating the amount of money it would have to sink into investments, Philips decided not to join a fight that for three years it dismissed as 'just a prestige contest'. Now Philips recognizes its mistake, but is afraid to take on all by itself the risk involved in attempting a full-scale recovery. Instead, it continues to build traditional electrical implements, and by taking the easier course threatens its world reputation as a technological leader in the industry.

In France the government, on the basis of reports submitted by a task force on industrial research, in 1966 gave top priority to a *plan-calcul* for coordinating and regrouping the three largest French electronic firms. French anxiety in this field may well be justified. In Germany, too, there is a new awareness of the problem, but their thinking and their operations have been limited to the national level. Siemens, their biggest electronics firm, recently announced a $125 million development budget for the period 1967–1970. Compare this to the $5 billion that IBM alone invested in the series 360 computer.

Such efforts by France and Germany, however useful psychologically or as short-term measures, do not have the slightest chance of bringing them up to the level of international competition. And their advocates know it. The French *plan-calcul*, in particular, does not even have such lofty ambitions. Its aim is simply to perfect medium-sized computers on which technicians, which we sadly lack at the moment, can be trained, and to create an Institute for Advanced Informational Studies where French engineers will be able to do basic research on software. This is a worthy ambition, but not equal to the problem, and one that leaves aside, at least for the time being, any attempt to create a European computer industry capable of competing with IBM or General Electric.

The British government has solemnly gone on record, through the Minister for Technology in the House of Commons, as declaring that 'At all cost Britain must maintain an independent and viable computer industry.' That was in 1966. Since then Britain has learned that she cannot pull this off by herself.

The Japanese acted quicker and with greater determination than the Europeans. They put rigid controls on computer imports to ensure that they do not exceed the number of Japanese-made machines. Also, they are developing an electrical parts industry that puts them just behind the United States in the production of integrated circuits. Experts believe that Japan's semi-dependence on the American computer industry is only a matter of a few years, and that by 1980 Japan will have won her independence in this area. This shows it can be done.

The logical policy for Europe would be to pool all the resources we can muster—probably from a British nucleus, with immediate support from German, French, and Dutch industry —into a unified effort, while blocking off some outlets for our own products. Only with a market of this size can we hope to compete with the Americans between now and 1980. This is a decision that must be made within the next few years.

Current disjointed, nearsighted attempts at competition by individual European governments are inexcusable, and doomed to failure. Not only can we succeed, we must succeed. No area of industry can ever be independent so long as we rely on others for computers. If there is a battle for the future, it is the battle of the computer.

CHAPTER 15

THE FRENCH EFFORT

In the confusion of today's Europe, France is the country that has shown the most determination not to become a satellite. Some of her reasons have been good, others more dubious. But her frame of reference has been almost entirely national.

What success has France had in this effort—carried out for political reasons we will not go into here—that she can hold up as an example to her partners? A joint study made by private industry and the French government tried to answer this question. Here are some of the major points of the unpublished report that came out of this inquiry.

The experts began by first posing the problem: 'In an international economy dominated by the United States, the progress of our industry depends above all on our capacity for invention, innovation, and technological change.'

Fact number one: Protected by tariff barriers, France has tried to produce everything and to export in every area, while operating from too small an industrial base and with outmoded methods. It is now obvious that the pace of foreign competition and the growth of foreign investment in France are taking place much faster than the modernization of French industry. French firms offer only a feeble resistance to the thrust of American capital.

Fact number two: The possession of raw materials has become a secondary factor in the economy of an industrialized country. The cost of raw materials is a diminishing proportion of the cost of the manufactured product. What counts today in the competition between nations is their technical capital, and even more importantly, their 'human capital'. A study by the

OECD shows that in terms of relative value, France exports an increasing amount of unfinished products. If the French continue to sell semi-manufactured products for raw materials, they will devalue their human capital and soon be flooded with finished products made elsewhere. France would be confined to the production of relatively primary goods involving little 'brain power'. Then, according to these experts, we might as well shut 'half our universities and tell our students to become apprentices.'

Third fact: The effort it would take to lift France to the level of a modern industrial country is not beyond her means; but it would threaten outdated businesses and methods hardened by custom and special privilege. Also, there are many sectors of the economy that are a drag on national progress and doomed by technological change, yet we continue to subsidize and develop them. In 1964 France spent 8½ billion francs ($1·7 billion) on subsidies to the railways, coal industry, shipyards, Parisian public transport, agriculture, etc. If a fraction of these 'subsidies to the past' were devoted to industrial research, France could greatly improve its competitiveness in industrial areas where innovation is crucial.

The total level of industrial research in France, public and private sectors included, is 5 billion francs ($1 billion) a year. A third of this goes into the public sector, and of that amount, 90 per cent is used by the military for the nuclear programme. Aside from research subcontracted to private industry, government research assistance is of two types: aid for development, and aid for joint projects between government and industry. The sums involved are almost ludicrous: 10 million francs ($2 million) in 1965 for the first, and less than 50 million francs for the second. Even if increased, as scheduled under the Fifth Economic Plan,[1] they are totally inadequate for a coherent research effort.

Not only are funds meagre, they are distributed badly. Aside from aviation and electronics, there are only 100 million francs to spread around the various competitive sectors. In 1964 the

[1] The *Plan* is a coordinated programme of long-term economic development drawn up by the French government in cooperation with nationalized industries, private business, trade unions, farm groups, management organizations, etc.

government worked out 104 joint projects with 48 companies for a total of 32 million francs, far below the amount needed for efficient operation and the development of markets.

In the United States nearly every major industry gets a substantial amount of federal assistance. Leaving aside space, aviation, and atomic energy, which we have already gone into, we can make the following comparison in other areas:

GOVERNMENT FINANCING IN CERTAIN INDUSTRIES

Industry	U.S.	France
Electrical and Electronic equipment	65 per cent	34·5 per cent
Automobiles	24 per cent	·5 per cent
Chemicals	20 per cent	2·5 per cent

French technicians who have drawn up these comparisons have shown how far we lag behind the United States even on a proportional basis. They have also pointed out that although France and Germany devote a similar percentage of their gross national product to industrial research, the level of military research is much lower in Germany—which puts France at an even greater disadvantage in civilian industrial research. Their conclusion is that French industry will be especially vulnerable to competition in the expanding market for technologically advanced products unless there is a massive infusion of funds into research and development.

The proportion of money going into research should be even greater than in the United States, since we have such a gap to fill. Considering the handicaps we are working under, we ought to be increasing our research expenditures at a much faster pace and, calculated as a proportion of our GNP, push them beyond the American level. But even under the most favourable circumstances, this goal can be achieved only if we accept far-reaching reforms—as we shall see.

These structural reforms are not a problem for economists to write about; they are a question of national policy, the management of French society, its domestic policy, and its ideological and moral choices (*see* chapters 21–24). Even supposing that the French can overcome these difficulties and make the effort to become really competitive, experts believe that the lag is already so great that the optimal level of funds for research and development lies beyond the nation's reach. The only hope, they believe, lies in what they circumspectly call 'integration in a wider economic area'. As far as development is concerned, this is already becoming obvious.

To achieve European integration every nation must prepare itself, and, above all, prepare its citizens. For France the objective for 1970 should be a level of industrial research equal (as percentage of GNP) to that of the United States, or 2·3 per cent, exclusive of government projects. Ideally it should be even more than that, but there is no point in demanding the impossible. If these objectives seem too ambitious, considering available resources and the political barriers that stand in the way, economists urge that by 1970 French industry should at least catch up to the British level of 1·6 per cent.

Phrasing it in this way, the problem is to determine how many scientists and technicians will have to be trained during the next three years. Estimates show that if France chooses the more ambitious goal, she will need 45,000 more in 1970 than she had in 1965; while if she shoots for the more modest British level, she will still need 27,000 more.

Her potential depends on several factors: the financial capacity of French industry, direct and indirect aid from the government, goals of the Fifth Economic Plan, availability of qualified labour; in short, the full management of French intellectual resources. Can enough scientists be trained?

According to the Fifth Plan and current forecasts of the number of graduates from the universities and junior colleges, 75,000 people will be trained as scientists during the duration of the Fifth Plan. Insofar as one can predict how they will be distributed, it seems likely that there would be between 12,500 and 17,500 new scientists going into industry. To reach the 17,500 figure would require a concentrated effort by both business and government; to exceed it would be to revise the whole basis of French economic planning.

Conclusion: in the framework of the present system of development, and the predicted growth rate, it will not be possible to attain the minimum (British) objective, let alone the optimal American one. While France has made a considerable financial effort in recent years, she is falling further behind the minimal threshold of industrial development in areas of advanced technology.

Even supposing the Plan fulfils all its goals, the total number of scientists in French industry in 1970 will be between 27,000 and 35,000. The corresponding research effort is thus only about 1 per cent of gross product, not counting government projects —far below what is needed to be competitive on the scientific front. To do better would require sweeping new plans, a radical transformation of training and management methods, a new sense of priorities, and cutting back on a number of wasteful projects that only dissipate our resources—in other words, a total change in objectives and ways of reaching them.

Of the six Common Market countries, France has been the most outspoken in her desire to escape American control. But without a larger European community offering them a different choice, the others seem resigned to economic dependency. The case of France thus furnishes a good example of the problem, and of the limits of a purely national effort at economic independence.

These limits seem so obvious that even the present French government has had to make some concessions to the theory of European unity, both by staying on board the Common Market ship and by joining its partners in such projects as Concorde or ELDO. But these gestures have not been much of an answer to the American challenge. The dynamism that should have taken the Six beyond the limitations of a simple Common Market has died out, and the institutions created in Brussels have begun to wither. They can be given new life only by going beyond them to build a *unified scientific and industrial policy*.

Everyone hoped that 'cooperative' projects, which would reconcile a respect for national sovereignty with the advantages of size, would offer a substitute. But paralysed by the doctrine of 'fair return' and by diplomatic manœuvrings, they are only a caricature of what should have been done.

Thus France and the other countries of Western Europe are going off simultaneously in three directions, but making no progress, unable to decide between the road of narrow nationalism, which is no longer passable; the road of cooperation, which goes nowhere; and the road of federation, which is blocked. Which road should we take?

PART 4

COUNTERATTACK

CHAPTER 16

BACK TO THE WALL

To regain control over our destiny in the face of the American challenge demands, as we have tried to show here, a new awareness among Europeans. Beyond that, as we will now try to describe, it will take long, hard work. What we must do is not so hard to put down on paper. The path of our counterattack is clearly marked:

1. Creation of large industrial units capable of competing with the American giants, both by their size and their management.

2. Carrying out 'major operations' of advanced technology that will insure an independent future for Europe.

3. At least a minimum of federal power to protect and promote European business.

4. Transforming the relationship between business, the university, and the government.

5. Broader and more intensive education for young people; specialized and continuing education for adults.

6. Finally, as the key to everything else, the liberation of imprisoned energies by a revolution in our methods of organization—a revolution to revitalize the elites and even relations between men.

This is an ambitious project, but a feasible one. Now we will try to sketch in how it can be put into practice.

If Europeans want to control their economic growth—and thereby their destiny—they can no longer afford the luxury of economic nationalism. An important book[1] has shown that the system we call socialism has little chance of achieving its effort

[1] *Le Socialisme et l'Europe* (Paris), (Club Jean Moulin, 1965).

to build a modern economy within the narrow framework of the medium-sized European state. This is true not only for socialism, but for any political system based on consent—of which socialism is one variety.

To build a powerful and independent Europe means strengthening the economic and political bonds of the Common Market. No single nation is strong enough to support efficient production in all the areas of advanced technology, for the national framework is too narrow and cannot provide adequate markets for such products. Also, the growing diversification of these products demands a specialization that makes any attempt at national self-sufficiency virtually impossible.

The national scale is too narrow even when the state moves in to support certain industries. Areas like scientific research, aviation, space, and computers go far beyond the narrow confines of a single medium-sized nation. If a country insists on getting along on its own national efforts, it either will dissipate its resources with little to show for it, as is the case with France and Britain, or it must concentrate its efforts on a few areas and not compete in others that are crucial to tomorrow's society, as Germany, Italy, and Belgium have done. This is why any attempt at economic self-reliance by the individual European nations would simply mean their abstention from technological progress, and a stagnation that would eventually become intolerable.

France, like her partners, is going to have to accept a degree of integration far greater than anyone ever imagined. This integration will be carried out by American big business if Europe does not do it herself. If the Europeans want to rely on the internal dynamics of the Common Market and the power of American industry, they can sit on the sidelines as their standard of living rises in an American-controlled world. During the colonial era the standard of living in colonies like Morocco and Madagascar was, in a similar way, gradually pulled up by France and French industrial development.

For the short run, the simplest solution would be to take the path of 'Atlanticism'. Plunging into an Atlantic framework would, for a time at least, allow us to overcome our economic limitations and participate in a general movement of economic progress. It would also, of course, prevent us from exercising any political control over our development, and would eventually lead to the stagnation that goes along with dependency (*see* chapter 4).

If Europeans want to control their economic growth, and thereby their future, they will have to create a geographic and human atmosphere broad enough to allow economic expansion, and to bring about the growth of private consumption, collective investment, and resources devoted to scientific and technological development.

The countries belonging to the European Community must coordinate their financial policy toward the same goals: we cannot be satisfied simply with a market, we must build an economic policy. Except for a withdrawal from the Common Market, which would lead to a rapid decline in our standard of living, economic planning on the national level is no longer possible. The member states of the Common Market have lost control over crucial areas of their economies, particularly those concerned with foreign trade, such as tariffs, import quotas, and exchange rates.

Our back is now to the wall. We cannot have both economic self-sufficiency and economic growth. Either we build a common European industrial policy, or American industry will continue taking over the Common Market. Since there is no longer any argument over the question of self-sufficiency and growth, it means we have to face some consequences in the field of action.

CHAPTER 17

BIGGER BUSINESS

INDUSTRY is what counts above all. But aside from liberalization in trade and agricultural policy, the Common Market has been preoccupied either with diplomatic crises or with relatively trivial economic questions. Year after year it has avoided the fundamental problems, those which call for difficult choices and bold solutions. Foremost of these problems is an industrial policy for Europe. Free trade is a framework, it is not a policy, nor is it a form of organization.

As Pierre Uri has written: 'The best answer to American investment is for Europe to unify its industries, encourage scientific research, and revise laws governing corporations. It is too easy to accuse others of imperialism when we fail to do what is necessary to avoid it.' What should we do? In a nutshell: achieve a real economic union and build giant industrial units capable of carrying out a global economic strategy.

Economic union is simple in theory. Everything has already been said about tax coordination and European corporate law. Everything, that is, except what is essential—that diplomatic delays in achieving these reforms run directly contrary to the major objective of the European Community, by leaving the initiative to American corporations. Beyond the obvious technical difficulties, there is a clear absence of a real political will. This can be felt on the most practical level. Should the Italian and the Belgian industrialists unite their businesses and operate on an international level? *They don't know.* They don't even know if it is legal. So they wait.

How can businessmen really believe they should stake their plans, their investments, indeed their whole future, on real

116

economic integration when the member states of the Common Market still show their politics by preparing and managing national budgets—where each country is concerned only with its own individual efforts, even for advanced research that clearly demands European unity? In the United States it is government contracts that act as a spur to technological innovation. Without a similar device in Europe there can be no serious answer to American investments. On the industrial level the Common Market is still only a tariff union. To make the jump to economic union is not only to change scope, but our priorities and our state of mind.

Today Europe is seriously outclassed in the four or five areas that hold the key to the future. Obviously Europeans ought to unite and concentrate their research and development efforts in these areas. But in the long run industrial policy can succeed only where it is rooted in an efficient and dynamic infrastructure of powerful and well-managed firms. During the past twenty years Britain has made an intense research effort, more than any other country in Europe. If this has not been rewarded by lasting success in the areas where it was concentrated, it is because Britain does not have industrial units comparable to the giant American corporations. And those that do have the size lack the dynamism.

The first problem of an industrial policy for Europe consists in choosing 50 or 100 firms which, once they are large enough, would be the most likely to become world leaders of modern technology in their fields. At the moment we are simply letting European industry be gradually destroyed by the superior power of American corporations. Counterattack requires a strategy based on the systematic reinforcement of those firms best able to strike back. *Only a deliberate policy of reinforcing our strong points*—what demagogues condemn under the vague term of 'monopolies'—*will allow us to escape relative underdevelopment.*[1] We need to unify European business, and we need to establish clear preferences. We have to begin with the

[1] This strategy will (rightly) seem dubious to those who mistrust the influence and political power of big business. This fear is justified. But the remedy lies in the power of government, not in the weakening of industry. We will try to expand on this subject in later chapters.

firms themselves, then move on to the separate European governments, and finally operate at the level of the Community.

The basic drive must come from the firms—from a determined will to grow and from implementing a strategy of innovation and progress. It is worth remembering the words of Mr. Cambien, when he observed that 'size is a means, not an end. The problem is not to change a brontosaurus into a dinosaur by doubling its size, but to form biological units adapted to new conditions of competition.'

At the national level, governments can increase their capacity for competition by providing investment funds, by fiscal policy, by enlightened research policy, and by development contracts. Yet current legislation in Western European countries poses almost insurmountable difficulties to business concentrations. Whether this involves actual mergers, partial ownership, or the creation of joint subsidiaries, the diversity of legal and fiscal systems in the various Common Market countries causes serious obstacles.

A study made in Brussels has detailed the problems faced by European firms when they try to unite their efforts. This survey[2] is an excellent dossier for labour leaders and politicians who really want to understand the paralysis that prevents European industry from unifying even if it wanted to, to confront the American offensive.

The problem is similar in the capital markets, as Dr. Rolfe[3] has shown in a convincing report. 'Most of the obstacles that fragment the European market,' he writes, 'come from the determination of financial authorities to maintain "stability" in terms of the balance of payments. Many industries, however, need extensive markets to provide them with capital. DuPont de Nemours, for example, could hardly exist if its borrowing power were limited to the financial markets of the state of Delaware, where it is incorporated. Commerce, industry, and finance are interconnected. Naturally there will be incongruity and conflict between a business of international scope and a financial market that is purely national. If European industry wants to compete with American industry as an equal, the

[2] *Etude de base sur les Marchés Financiers*, Brussels, January 1967.

[3] *Capital Markets in Atlantic Economic Relationships*.

European financial markets will have to be integrated.' In this field an important step was taken in 1966–1967 to free the movement of capital; now we have to overcome the inertia of old habits.

On the level of European Community, top priority for action is in the field of corporate law. Under present conditions, mergers of firms in different countries involve such losses for stockholders—as a result of taxes imposed on non-residents, or double taxation, or inequity in the tax laws—that the law poses a formidable obstacle to the concentration of industry. In any case, this is its effect.

Before leaving this problem of building big industrial units, we should deal briefly with the British question.[4] Among all the countries of Europe, Britain has the greatest number of firms of international scope, and the most extensive research programme. Among the 500 largest corporations in the world, Britain is right behind the United States, with 55 firms. Germany, by contrast, has only 30, France 23, and Italy 8.

Among firms doing more than $250 million worth of business a year, 8·4 per cent are British, compared to 6·3 per cent for Germany, 3·3 per cent for France, 1·6 per cent for Italy, and 1·4 per cent for the Benelux countries. Comparing the level of industrial research, Britain alone conducts an amount equal to 60 per cent of the total of all the Common Market countries combined.

It is worth noting that Britain concentrates her efforts on electronics, electrical equipment, nuclear energy, and aviation— that is, on those very areas that the European Community should be developing to compete with the United States. Britain would be the *best possible ally* for France within the Common Market. She could help endow Europe with a world role, and save her from becoming a giant Switzerland.

[4] Obviously these few paragraphs do not pretend to deal with the question of Britain's entry into the Common Market. If we have not spent several chapters on the subject, it is because this is a political, and not an economic, problem. Britain's place is clearly within the Common Market.

CHAPTER 18

MAJOR OPERATIONS

DEVOTING a reasonable part of our national product for the great industrial battle is not enough. We must make some hard choices. It will be a long time before European research and development is able to compete effectively with the United States in all major areas.

What we should try to do is achieve breakthroughs in certain fields of advanced technology. This is what French and European experts call *les grandes operations*, or major operations— those that by their dynamism, their scope, and their scientific importance can stimulate our whole economy.

A major operation should shake up a thousand routine ways of doing things, bring together industrial teams whose paths otherwise never cross, unleash a hurricane of studies, discoveries, and products from a single exciting idea. Caught up in this spirit, the best firms will be able to form high-quality research teams, accumulate new skills and knowledge, expand their creative potential, invent new products, and open up new markets.

There is a vast field for such operations. Every year there are new discoveries that seem to come straight from the realm of science-fiction. But they are expansive and getting more so all the time. Even if its economy were rationalized and reorganized, Europe would not be fully competitive on all fronts by 1980. Nor, for that matter, can any country in the world, including the United States, be totally independent. We are developing an international division of labour based on competition. The objective is not to be self-sufficient in every industrial area, but

120

to be strong enough in certain advanced areas to compel the respect of rivals.

The success of a major operation depends, of course, on having firms big enough to be competitive. But that is not enough. An effective campaign requires massive and sustained government aid. In Europe, as in the United States, such a government must be federal.[1]

Those working out the strategy of counterattack have developed two other plans of action to back up the major operation: one which groups together 'small skirmishes' (medium-sized and small firms), and the other which concerns 'scattered research' (funds spread out over a number of small projects). Working out a chart for these three plans of action, it would seem that our efforts should be divided in these proportions: 75 per cent for the major campaign, 15 per cent for the small skirmishes, and 10 per cent for scattered research. This underlines the importance of the major campaign, which is the gateway to the future for our generation.

Today in France there are three embryonic major operations that can be expanded: space research, atomic energy, and supersonic aviation. The U.S. lead in these three fields is so great that any attempt to catch up by a single nation, such as France, Britain, or Germany, would be a waste of money. But we could catch up in all three of these areas if we united our forces. If the Europeans concentrated their efforts they could, by 1980, make a showing in space without using American satellites, build nuclear power plants that can match the

---

[1] In the next chapter we will examine the necessary limitations of federalism.

[2] We have not elaborated the problem of atomic energy in order not to make a long technical dossier even longer, and also because the problem is fairly well understood.

Europe is, or at least was, competitive with the United States in the field of atomic energy for civilian use. With fewer sources of natural energy at their disposal than the United States, the European countries started to build nuclear power centres at an early date, and by 1960 had twice as many as the United States. Since then the situation has been reversed. Why? Again the same reasons: development studies, market studies, concentration of resources, and technological alternatives.

American-made ones in price,[2] and compete with the U.S. on the supersonic civilian aeroplane market.

Unless we abandon all efforts to become independent, we Europeans cannot neglect any of these three crucial areas, except perhaps aviation, if worse comes to worse. But there is no question of abstaining from competition in space and in nuclear energy. These fields are so important that they justify, and even necessitate, pooling our efforts, achieving at least a minimum of federalism, and mobilizing our men and resources against the American monopoly.

But as important as these areas are, they are less crucial than the fourth area of electronics. Europeans dealing with these problems have made the following diagnosis: 'Development of the electronics industry controls productivity and the modernization of the whole framework of industry and services. Because of the importance of electronics in stimulating progress in every area of human activity, and because European industrial support, even though not comparable to that of the United States, could reach the competitive level, we must prepare for a great expansion in this area. During the years ahead the expansion of electronics will be centred in the development of information systems, such as computers and teletransmitters.'

Economists believe that European branches of firms like IBM and General Electric pose an opportunity as well as a

---

Atomic energy has a future only if it is less expensive than combustible fuels. One of the objectives of Euratom was to rationalize the development of atomic energy in Europe to avoid duplication and produce it at a competitive price. The total failure of Euratom has left France, Germany, and Britain to pursue their separate, expensive, ineffective programmes in competition with the co-ordinated effort of the United States.

Americans have been able to produce atomic power plants at a reasonable price for industry, while Europeans have not. By 1967 the former ratio had been reversed, with Europe producing 43 plants and the United States 74.

Atomic energy in the future will be based on super-generators capable of extracting fifty times more energy from a ton of uranium than existing atomic piles. Europe's problem is to unify and rationalize her research and development programmes for super-generators. At the moment these programmes are in competition with one another, thus leaving the field free to American technology.

danger, for they stimulate new projects and encourage the training of scientists and engineers in our universities. They also encourage the creation of a whole set of subsidiary industries that will be useful to the development of European information techniques. And they goad us on to rally our forces for the success of the major operations.

But since the individual electronics firms of Europe are so much smaller than the American giants, they will need massive government support to catch up. No European computer industry will be profitable for a good many years. Even in the United States the biggest electronics firms have not always been able to make a profit during the past decade. Electronics is clearly an area where cooperation between business and government will be indispensable for many years to come.

If the French *plan-calcul* has been built on too narrow a base, it nonetheless remains valid as a strategy for a European-scale *plan-calcul*. Business and government in both Britain and Germany have contacted the French to set up a common plan. The major obstacle is neither financial nor technical, but political. To build a truly integrated European *plan-calcul* without national secrecy or the disastrous principle of 'fair return', and with the necessary unified command, would be to achieve federalism in industry. That is precisely the choice: either an all-European *plan-calcul* with all the reconversions it will require, or domination by IBM. There is not much time left to choose, if we want to have some independence by 1980.

Once we have defined our course of action, chosen our campaign, and forged links between industry and government, we then have to organize a new set of relations for the 'business-university-government complex'. According to French officials: 'We must establish contact, on the one hand, between universities and the CNRS (National Center for Scientific Research), which furnish ideas and scientists, and on the other hand, with businessmen who turn research into concrete products. That is the basic problem, and in its solution lies the success of all the efforts we must undertake to encourage effective industrial research. Yet under present conditions there is no connection between the two.' If there is to be any collaboration, there will have to be considerable changes on both sides.

We must, first of all, develop 'customer-supplier' relations:

both government and university research laboratories must consider it natural to work under contract on projects determined by industry. There must also be a better understanding of the 'committee-boss' relationship. While the choice of an industrial objective may well come out of a committee meeting of civil servants, scientists, and businessmen, there can be only a single authority once the objective has been decided upon. This 'boss' is responsible for the entire operation, however large it may be, and must have considerable freedom of action and decision-making power. The committee-boss relationship is badly understood in Latin countries, and particularly in France. A close association between business, university, and the government has never been perfected nor successful in any European country.

Yet this is the basic secret of the American success story. Adapting it to Europe will be even harder than dealing with our financial and technical problems, for it demands a radical change in our attitude and way of doing things. But it could also be the most rewarding.

Building bigger business units and carrying out large-scale projects means we must unify our legal and fiscal rules governing corporations, deliberately choose which industries should grow and which should be allowed to die out, pursue vigorous development in the areas of advanced technology, and combine the efforts of industry, the universities, and government.

Who will be the judge of these choices? The person who takes charge of the operations? Who will be responsible to businessmen, civil servants, and professors for the wisdom of these choices?

It would be foolish to count on a natural identity of interests, on the conciliatory skills of diplomats, or on spontaneous harmony in these various areas. To solve problems of this scope men long ago invented something called political authority. Only the communist society described by Karl Marx has no need for it. But such a society does not exist. Elementary logic, freed from any a priori dogma, suggests that Europeans must accept a minimum of federal power if they want their societies to survive. There is nothing particularly mysterious about this, and nothing to excite wild passion or fear—as we will now try to show.

CHAPTER 19

A MINIMUM OF FEDERALISM

To see what a European counterattack means for the individual nation-states, we ought to take a look at our neighbours. On the fringes of the Common Market are the seven nations belonging to EFTA.[1] These nations have very much the same ideas as France about their foreign economic policy. By joining the Common Market and entering the Kennedy Round, France showed that she favours free exchange. So do the EFTA countries. France is opposed to giving up her sovereignty, and refuses to accept common economic policies for industry, science, etc. So do they. Isn't this reasonable?

These countries are right, being what they are; and we are wrong, being what we are. Except for a single case, as we shall see, the EFTA countries are right in holding to their present position, for it is based on a long tradition of narrow economic specialization—as illustrated by Sweden and Switzerland. None of them wants to play the role of a great power. Their economic policy is consistent with their size and their limited ambitions.

Of all the EFTA countries, only Britain has been haunted by the kind of ghosts that have troubled France. Britain wanted to build an economic and technological organization worthy of her past; but she refused to dilute her sovereignty in a political community. She is now burdened with a stagnant economy and policies that stimulate unemployment.

Here is a country that ought to enter the Common Market, for the rules of the free trade zone forbid any common economic policy that would favour Britain's ambitions. The British are in

[1] European Free Trade Association, which links Britain to Austria, Denmark, Norway, Sweden, Switzerland, and Portugal.

a good position to understand this, and the first suggestion they made in seeking entry to the Common Market was the creation of a European technological community—which is hardly possible without at least a minimum of federalism.

Sweden, Switzerland, and Austria are right, and we are wrong, for we are trying to be a world power, and we have done nothing to achieve some kind of specialization. To try to do so now would be useless. It would require numerous firms in whole areas of our economy to shut down to make room for more competitive firms in areas with high priority. This would be politically painful and socially intolerable. The road taken by Sweden or Switzerland is not open to France. If this road is closed and we want to avoid American domination, the only road left open—as the British have found out (and they were even more opposed to it than we)—is through federalism.

The rules of federalism will not be easy to accept, for they are bound to be harsh. But we must not lose sight of the objective of becoming competitive with the United States. While the Europe of the Six has nearly the same population as the United States, it is technologically and financially much weaker. If the situation were reversed, we could get by with a weaker organization that would allow us to make an easier transition. But to rouse Europe from her present inferiority and restore her to independence means that we must build a powerful and effective European organization.

Pierre Mendes-France, a respected French political figure who can hardly be suspected of a doctrinnaire prejudice for supranationality, has declared: 'We must give the institutions of the European Community the authority, the means, and the resources to build a real community capable of adjusting the interests of the member states. This policy is essential if Europe is to be independent of the United States.'

An editorial in *The Observer* of London has added: 'The only hope for bridging the growing technological gap between Europe and America is to build a strong central authority capable of studying markets and resources, and then deciding where Europeans should concentrate their efforts. It must be strong enough to resist the pressure of national and international lobbies, and have sufficient funds to carry out its projects.'

The two conditions necessary for an efficient European

organization are, first, authority in certain areas over the individual nation-states, and, second, its own financial resources so that it can carry out large-scale projects agreed upon jointly. Since these conditions are often complicated by polemics, we shall try to clarify them.

The first condition, authority, raises the question of majority rule. There are two major methods for forging political links between states: confederation and federation. ELDO furnishes an exemple of the *confederal* system. The basic criterion is that decisions must be made by unanimous vote. This means that the only communal institution is a secretariat, which has a certain limited power over the way decisions are applied, but none at all over the decisions themselves. Such institutions act slowly, badly, and feebly, for they are obliged to work out compromises between divergent national interests rather than to make decisions based on the common interest. Big industrial projects can never be conceived and carried out in this way.

The other kind of organization is *federal*, and rests on the principle that a majority (either simple or absolute) can decide certain issues. Any federation thus has certain residual powers of its own, and its various organizations are directed by men who are responsible to the federal authority.

The difference between a confederation and a federation is not one of degree, but of kind. It can even be said that the latter is the antithesis of the former. In a confederation all decisions must be unanimous, which means that they never reach very far or very deep. Hobbled by its rule of unanimity, confederation encourages abstention rather than action, and, to use the vocabulary of economics, free trade rather than joint policies, laissez-faire rather than decisive action.

If, on the other hand, members of a community agree to reach certain decisions by majority vote, action becomes much simpler. Everyday experience shows that no company, trade union, club, or even family, for that matter, can function without some form of majority rule. *Unanimity is a formula for negation; majority rule a formula for action.* To want the Common Market without accepting majority rule is to seek a utopian society where there is no authority. It is to make a vacuum of the power renounced by the member states when they agreed to eliminate trade barriers, and to do so at the very moment when we are confronted by a formidable American challenge.

Even trade liberalization will be stopped short of its goal if we cannot work out a minimal common policy. There can be no Common Market in fuel, for example, if the Six cannot agree on a common energy policy. We have already seen how the Coal and Steel treaty has been emasculated. If trade liberalization should cause serious problems for some region or economic sector of a member state, as is virtually inevitable, that state would feel obliged to defy the Treaty of Rome and impose restrictive measures—if there were no common policy to prevent it. Other states would have to retaliate, and in doing so would imperil the major accomplishment of the past decade—trade liberalization, which is the key to growth.

Now let us look at the problem of resources. Why has the United States made the most extraordinary technological breakthrough in the history of the world, all in the past ten years? Primarily because the U.S. government has helped pay for giant projects that turn the discoveries made by what Americans call 'Big Science' into manufactured industrial products. Behind most of their recent innovations is a huge reservoir of federal funds that have financed the most profitable investment any people ever made for itself.

If we want to compete with the Americans and build a technology as powerful as theirs, we will have to give the Common Market the financial power that will allow it to play the same role as the U.S. federal budget. This cannot be done by contributions from the separate nation-states, since this would only involve Europe in perpetual quarrels, contracts of convenience, and diplomatic marathons. To accept majority rule in certain special cases is to admit that there can be a legitimate political authority superior to the nation-state. To endow this authority with its own financial power is to accept a kind of federalism.

It would be shortsighted and hypocritical to say that we will move smoothly from today's confederal Europe—which has to make its decisions unanimously and has almost no money for development—to the kind of Europe we ought to have if we want to compete with American industry. European economic power is not growing, but is actually deteriorating. Neither

Europe nor France can escape American 'colonization' until our present political structure is replaced by a European federation, which obviously must rest on a foundation of democracy and universal suffrage.

While their freedom of action may be limited in the beginning, the first leaders of a federated Europe will have the power to decide whether we will rise or decline. Those who must build this new power, make its weight felt, and use its influence to arbitrate will have to rely on the only source of political legitimacy that counts, universal suffrage. No matter how capable technocrats may be, they can never marshal the authority to push the common interest over parochial interests. In order to succeed we will need elected leaders capable of mobilizing public opinion and speaking to the peoples of Europe over the heads of their conservative ruling groups. It does not matter whether we elect a European parliament, or more likely, a federal assembly, as in Switzerland. This last solution is probably the more reasonable, but what is important is that, one way or another, we achieve an act of federalism.

Let's consider a recent example. There is a single field, and only one, where the Six have temporarily delegated authority to a Community body—when they allowed the Commission in Brussels to represent them in the Kennedy Round. While these states have very different basic interests from one another, they impressed everyone with their ability to work out a common strategy in the spring of 1967 to deal with the Americans in the tough Kennedy Round negotiations. The *Financial Times* of London remarked that the success of the European negotiators was 'due to the aggressive attitude of the Commission toward the United States.' This was a demonstration of federalism par excellence. As Aurelio Peccei, one of the great Italian industrialists later commented: 'If we can get rid of the idea of the nation-state, I see a brilliant intellectual and psychological recovery for us.'

Obviously there are risks involved in European federation. What comes of it will be, as always, what men make of it. But to refuse to take this risk is to deprive ourselves of any possibility of effectively facing the American challenge. To refuse the minimum amount of federalism necessary for a joint economic policy is to have no economic policy at all. This is to play the game of whatever power is dominant, and submit ourselves to its strategy.

We should take a closer look at what federalism really means, for the risks are not nearly so great as we may imagine. France has opted for free trade, and got it. But the constraints imposed on our sovereignty by trade liberalization are much greater than those that would result from joining a European federation. This point is basic, for everything else follows from it.

While free trade is necessary to economic growth, it involves serious outside restraints on our currency, our budget, our prices, and our monetary policy. If the liberalization of trade is not accompanied by joint policies, these restraints are imposed upon us by blind market forces over which we have no control. We are at the mercy of big business, market-sharing and cartels, and American industrial power.

It is a mistake to think that political federation could threaten our national identity. Some people imagine that if we had real European federalism, the Paris chief of police could be a German or an Italian. This is to forget that federations, by definition, are always limited in their authority, and are obliged to respect regional differences—and obviously national identities as well.

Nearly two centuries after its establishment, the U.S. federal government is incapable of enforcing civil rights legislation in certain Southern states. Even Kennedy's assassins were not judged in Washington, but in Dallas, and under circumstances that are all too familiar. These are the actual limitations of a powerful and long-standing political federation. To imagine that a European political federation would force the French, for example, to abandon their centralized system of education is quite illusory, when one recalls that in the German Federal Republic the various *Lander*, or provinces, unfortunately control their own educational systems.

Then what does federalism really involve? Simply the transfer from the national level to the European level of a *very small number of problems* that cannot be efficiently handled by individual nation-states. Above all, it means forging a scientific and industrial policy capable of dealing with the United States.

Like any decision about the future, federalism involves many risks and uncertainties. But these risks are limited, and the only absolute risk is to deprive ourselves of the means to respond when the danger is so pressing. How can we act? We have to search further.

CHAPTER 20

HEART OF THE MATTER

BETTER organization would be reason enough to justify a European federation, for our recovery hinges on the creation of a federal authority. But there are other reasons. Aside from the technical problems that stand in the way of recovery, a kind of inhibition paralyses the countries of Europe and their leaders.

This feeling of impotence can be seen in the resignation of those who have submitted to American domination, and in the anger of those who reject it but don't know what to do about it. So long as such a paralysis threatens our ancient civilization, the ingenuity of experts is not much help. What we need is a political jolt to bring us back to health.

Political action offers a freedom that technicians almost never have. Politics can change the course of national destiny by awakening dormant forces and organizing scattered interests. When Churchill took over from Chamberlain in 1940, Britain turned away from appeasement and became a nation of courage. By itself a political act can free aspirations trapped in confining, antiquated social structures. To understand what such an act can mean, we ought to take a hard look at the forces working against it.

In this task we have the help of Michel Crozier, one of the finest young French sociologists. Here are some of his conclusions from a paper presented at a colloquy held in Rome.[1]

Our object is to analyse the attitudes of different European leadership groups towards affecting their future problems. This

[1] International seminar on 'European leadership groups and the problems of national and international operations'. Text translated from the Italian.

question has been dealt with in terms of economic development and new aspects of management. Surveys of public opinion have also been made. But so far there has been no successful effort to delve deeply into the workings of the political-social systems in the various European countries. This process, which is so difficult to change, must be the source and the objective of European development. And it is these difficulties that European firms are now struggling with.

One of the basic elements of this problem is the way the leadership groups react. When we speak of changing the general atmosphere or the direction in which our societies are moving, we put great emphasis on the evolution of attitudes and opinion. While this is important, it is not enough. No one can predict decisions from a study of attitudes. Rather, it is easier to gauge basic attitudes from decisions, once the decisions are made. Studies in experimental and social psychology show that the crucial factor is the decision. This is a function of a complex process we must try to understand.

These reflections can be divided into two topics:

1. The importance of the *challenge* facing our societies because of economic, social, and technological evolution. This challenge has dramatized the difficulties facing every European country as it tries to cope with problems that exceed its capacity.

2. The second topic is the *rigidity* of European society. For the most part our systems are too 'coherent', and give the impression of working within a framework that traps them.

European societies manifest this sense of impotence in several ways: by loss of their creative drive; by the feeling of no longer being in the running, of having dropped out of the race for scientific and sociological developments that determine our form of civilization; and by the conviction that they have been outpaced and are no longer able to compete in the areas that count for human progress.

Among those who stress the economic situation, our Belgian friends cite examples of the importance of American investment in the development of the Belgian economy. They tell us that these investments are the basic reason for industrial growth in Belgium. Since everyone agrees on the technological and scientific lag of the European countries, let's consider this point more closely.

There is a good deal of European capital in Europe, but only American firms seem to profit from it. Why? This is the problem, and it cannot be phrased only in economic terms. It involves our capacity for organization: the ability to work under different conditions, to take advantage of an enormous market, to know how to make a profit from it and adapt to its needs. Europe's lag seems to concern *methods of organization* above all. The Americans know how to work in our countries better than we do ourselves.

This is not a matter of 'brain power' in the traditional sense of the term, but of organization, education, and training. We have men capable of carrying out research, but we do not have organizations that can develop this research on a large enough scale to succeed in today's world. Our universities are ossified and inadequate, and it is extremely difficult to change them.

Thus the problem is to transform the whole system: business, intellectual talent, education, research. So far our efforts have been misdirected. We have tried to build production centres, but too often they have been only agglomerations of production, financially centralized, but as badly managed as the collection of individual firms that form them. This is no way to build more aggressive, development-conscious organizations.

In the field of education, and particularly in higher education, there have been in France, for example, reforms in several areas, but they are so confined by the rigidity of the old system that they are unlikely to have a lasting success. We can make changes in certain sectors and create new systems, but in the end, the old traditions stand firm and the basic structure itself remains outdated.

The reports presented in this seminar stress the chasm between social life (the daily life of the individual) and political society (the government and the ruling elite). We have observed that our social life is changing in the direction of the American model. Yet European leadership groups do not seem to have grasped this evolution, nor do they want to.

Why such a divorce between social life and political society? We will answer with a hypothesis: what is most striking is not the apparently irreversible evolution towards a consumer's society without humanistic vision, but the absence of the authority and the influence of leadership groups. This absence of authority seems to come from rigidity and from a curious desire by these leaders to sit on the sidelines of change.

If the relationship between the leadership groups and the people is so weak, it is because these groups remain hobbled by their outdated views, traditional ideals, and old methods of exerting pressure. The old methods, bureaucratic and aristocratic in nature, are the same ones by which they are trying to act today. But they are totally inappropriate to the new society now being formed. From this comes the sense of impotence and abnegation.

The second theme concerns the rigidity of national systems. It is interesting to analyse the difference of tone between reports presented by Belgium and Holland on one hand, and by France, Britain, and Germany on the other, with Italy somewhere in the middle.

The French, British, and German reports reveal the closed character of the systems represented by various individuals and leadership groups. These reports stress beginnings, and possibilities of change, but almost immediately fall back on a kind of automatic 're-nationalism' that has always been there. The proof of this can be seen in the success of the Fifth Republic's foreign policy. Because nationalism is so strong in France, it was only when relations with the European community began to influence the French administration that the administration dug in its heels against it. What is now taking place on the political level stems from this kind of reaction. Nor is this an accident. This reaction corresponds to the stability of the French socio-political equilibrium. This stability is different from that in Belgium, for example, because in France the government plays a more important role. The complex manœuvres of the French system take place around the state and its administration.

French political leaders, economists, workers, and farmers have been interviewed on regional problems. It is clear that all of them—theoretically victims of the government which they feel exploits them—are strongly attached to the system. We were surprised by the candour with which they declared they would rally around the prefect when there is an important decision to be made.

A similar vicious circle, under a different form, traps the

Belgians and the Dutch into groups divided by religious and political passions. These divisions operate as a powerful armour against efforts at change. In France the strength of the system can be seen in the way every union member, or employer, or regional group believes that the answer to every problem lies in the administrative apparatus of the government.

The report on Germany shows that each party and political group tries to adapt and move ahead so that it can communicate within a European framework. But they remain essentially unchanged because they are confined by nationalism.

These observations can be summarized by stating that European society today is closed and stratified, and that the evolution towards the mass-consumption society escapes control by the ruling elite just as it does by the government, for they are both currently incapable of mobilizing the resources necessary for the development of a truly European community.

This development is now taking place in a passive fashion, for *there is no leadership to give it life and turn it into an active type of development* in which the vast majority of the population could take part. We continue to suffer progress rather than pursue it.

A solution will not be easy, for it demands and implies positive action. Everything is rooted in the socio-cultural problem. The adaptation of leadership groups, or elites, is generally passive, and even reactionary. Remarkable means of action such as television and other forms of mass communication, and technological developments now at the disposal of education, have been ignored by the elites even as they complain about the way the masses are becoming 'Americanized'.

Thus our problems are rooted in the need to change the hopelessly ossified European societies which find it so difficult to become more flexible.

This is particularly true for the French. Every time it seems possible to make a decisive break with the old system, they draw back in alarm.

This is today's Europe as it confronts the challenge of growth, the challenge of power. This is the heart of the matter. It is not a problem of numbers, but of the minds of men. What political forces, what ideas, what men can open them to change?

PART 5

THE POLITICAL QUESTION

CHAPTER 21

THE CHOSEN GENERATION

THE postwar generation was faced with the choice of seeing all Europe unified within the communist world or of trying to maintain an independent Western Europe. Today's generation faces a less dramatic, but equally clear choice of building an independent Europe or letting it become an annex of the United States. The sheer weight of American power is pushing our hesitant countries along the path of annexation, and the point of no return may be reached before today's ten-year-olds are able to vote.

It is still possible for us to catch up, but there is a great deal of dead weight to overcome. This does not mean we have to make real sacrifices, for by trying to become her own mistress, Europe will increase her power and wealth, and finally the well-being of her citizens. But perhaps it is asking too much of Europeans to adapt to global competition, shake themselves loose from entrenched national habits, pull together dispersed resources, adjust to severe new rules of management, and stop wasting precious men and capital. Is it reasonable to ask an old continent to show the vitality of a new nation—especially when the satellization of Europe is accompanied, at least initially, by a rising standard of living and by only a very gradual reduction of our freedom of thought? Our dependence will not stop Frenchmen from discussing politics or Germans from going to the opera. Why, then, try to oppose it?

Western Europeans look on self-determination as an acquired right; they cannot imagine it could really be threatened. Man's right to determine the shape of his society and his future seems entirely natural—and with good reason. The principle of self-determination was born in Europe, introduced during a time of slavery in ancient Greece, taken up by the more enlightened theology of the Middle Ages and the Renaissance, put into practice by England, the 'mother of parliaments', proclaimed by the French Revolution, and extended to economics through the inspiration of socialism.

It was first applied in the favoured zones of the northern hemisphere, where less than a fifth of the world's population lives. Democracy might seem to be the result of chance, if history had not proved that it was an *idée fixe*, a central element of all the principles that have shaped European thought—and one strong enough, at least until now, to survive catastrophes and fraud. This desire for self-determination, for freedom first from physical oppression, then from social restraints, is a hallmark of our civilization.

The day this drive weakens to the point that Europeans let 'somebody bigger' do their work for them, the spirit of our civilization will have broken, as did that of the Arab and Indian civilizations centuries ago. We would be tainted by the knowledge of our own failure. Without suffering from poverty, we would nevertheless soon submit to a fatalism and depression that would end in impotence and abdication.

There is no way of leaving the 'economic area' to the Americans so that we can get on with political, social, and cultural areas in our own way, as some people would like to believe. There is no such compartmentalization in the real world. Naturally there will not be any 'American committee' to administer Europe, as Paul Valéry imagined. Citizens would continue to vote, trade unions could strike, and parliaments to deliberate. But it will all take place in a vacuum. With our growth rate, our investment priorities, and the distribution of our national income determined by the United States, it is not even necessary to imagine secret meetings between Wall Street bankers and European cabinet ministers to understand that the areas that really count would lie outside the democratic process.

The European elite would be trained at Harvard, Stanford, or Berkeley, continuing a precedent that has already begun. This elite would no doubt worm itself into a kind of Atlantic oligarchy, and even gain some influence over its decisions. But this would only raise another barrier between the governors and the governed: the aptitude for American *savoir-faire* and *savoir-vivre* would bestow privileges as great as those that now go with a degree from the École Polytechnique or Oxford.

A few leading firms, subsidiaries of American corporations, would decide how much European workers would earn and how they would live—work methods, human relations on the job, standards for wages and promotion, and job security. Employers, whether European or American, would be little more than clerks, enjoying some powers of initiative, but only within a framework worked out by the parent company and laid down to its subsidiaries around the world.

American capital and American management will not stop short at the gates of our society. No favours of the sacred will keep these managers from crossing the threshold of the European sanctuary. They will take a majority interest in, and then control, the firms that dominate the market in publishing, the press, gramophone recording, and television production. The formulas, if not all the details, of our cultural 'messages' would be imported. Our system of education—in the large sense of channels of communication by which customs are transmitted and ways of life and thought formulated—would be controlled from the outside.

Cairo and Venice were able to keep their social and cultural identities during centuries of economic decline. But it was not such a small world then, and the pace of change was infinitely slower. A dying civilization can linger for a long time on the fragrance left in an empty vase. We will not have that consolation.

If France and Germany were really able to exercise the same rights as the state of New York or California, if Frenchmen and Germans could become 'full-fledged citizens' of the American federation, our abdication would not be so great. We could then take part in the exercise of this world power, and while we sacrificed national identity, we would not also have to sacrifice self-government. But the American republic is a finished product. If Americans wanted to, they still could not change the federal system laid down in the Constitution. It is too late to contemplate such a solution. Even if a transatlantic union could maintain the essential principle of self-determination, Europeans would find the desire to preserve their own differences was reason enough to remain separate.

Some of our characteristics stem, it is true, from a simple technological lag. Many signs of 'Americanization' are really indications of a change that Europe would have gone through by herself if the United States were dragging up the rear instead of leading the way. The hatred and fear of America felt by many Europeans is really their own fear of a future that was chosen by their fathers when they launched the first industrial revolution, and which they themselves re-affirmed by starting the second. But what makes Europe unique cannot be explained by a simple time lag.

Like many enlightened Americans today, Europeans have tried, in many cases successfully, to limit the power of money over the life of man. Despite prosperity, a man's income is not the same thing as his prestige; the most expensive medical care is available to the most impoverished; community needs and social services that cannot be bought on the market are better provided in Europe. Part of the Negro problem in the United States comes from a failure to recognize that this social fabric, while expensive, has a powerful ability to knit together individuals within a society.

It is often said that respect for intelligence and the protection of individuals from conformist pressures of society are historically linked to the feudal, or aristocratic, class structure of yesterday's Europe. But as Stanley Hoffman has said, 'there is no reason for giving up either. On the contrary, it is a reason for trying to adapt both to the age of democracy. All individuals, not just an elite, ought to be shown how to escape from the alienation of labour, from enslavement to technology, and from the shrill demands of the mass media, of the neighbours, or of all sorts of groups.'

There is no excuse for Europeans to be passive or complacent, for they are free to examine the American experience critically, to make of tomorrow's Europe 'an industrial society that will have its own profile, not simply because many of the old features will not have been erased by the plastic surgery of industrialization, but also because of a deliberate effort to preserve Europe's originality.'[1]

Will Europe, with infinitely greater means, resources, and

[1] Stanley Hoffmann, professor Harvard University, 'Europe's Identity Crisis', *Daedalus* (Fall 1964), pp. 1270, 1271.

power, be incapable of attempting as a world power what Sweden has done by specializing in a few areas? With the highest standard of living in the world (after the United States), this country of 8 million people has maintained its own identity —one sharply different from that of the United States. In Sweden they tear down old-age homes in perfectly good condition because advances in geriatrics allow society to offer something better to older people. This concern for non-commercial values has not prevented Sweden from producing highly competitive goods in certain carefully chosen areas.

The experience of Japan, while rather different, leads to a similar conclusion: economic growth can be adapted to social behaviour and concepts of society far removed from the American model. Growth is compatible with a great variety of social institutions and individual behaviour. 'The power of Japan's example is not that it encourages us to imitate her society, but to accept a cultural relativism that allows each country to sink the roots of industrialization and economic progress into its own history.'[2] Varying balances can then be worked out between initiative and security, individual consumption and community development, private power and public power. A nation that is master of itself is free to stamp its own mark on society.

If Europe decides to do this, she would greatly improve the chances of building a decent world, one that could reconcile the unity of modern industrial society with the variety of national cultures that compose it. A polycentric world would ensure a growing exchange of goods and ideas, and the continuing competition between human societies that has always been the condition of human progress. Would an isolated Egypt, Greece, or Rome have done any better than the Mayas trapped in their jungle?

An independent Europe is essential for orderly world economic development. Is there any group of advanced nations— other than those of the Common Market, together with Britain —that could form a pole of attraction different from both America and Russia? A united Europe could bring about significant changes in the world power balance, and not only from the strength of her ideas. They would come, above all, from the very

---

[2] Hubert Brochier, *Le Miracle économique japonais* (1967).

creation of a third great industrial power with no imperial
pretensions—one whose only strategy is to help build a more
unified international community.

Some might say that this is pure utopianism. While such a
project is feasible, it requires an intellectual leap into the future
over a thousand discouraging obstacles. It demands a choice of
principles that cannot be justified in terms of pure efficiency.
To take this gamble we have to rid ourselves of scepticism. We
have to realize that the nation-state is not the ultimate form of
social organization and that politics is more than the short-term
adjustment of power and of interest groups. According to a
study made by Herman Kahn (see chapter 3) of the world 30
years from now, *it is unlikely that the European countries will
make this effort, this leap into a higher form of civilization*, and
it does not enter into his predictions.

'It does not seem likely to this writer,' he states, 'that the
kinds of challenges and choices with which Europe will actually
be presented in the next decade or two are likely to lead to any
rapid movement toward unification. Under foreseeable circumstances the special situation of the Europeans in possessing a
Common Market will not necessarily lead them to forge political
institutions capable of centralized decision-making. Europe is
likely to have a relatively low morale insofar as projecting her
objectives on the world scene.

'The emergence of Japan and China may, in fact, force the
large European nations to accept a status of fifth, sixth, or
seventh in the international hierarchy during the last decades of
this century. But this loss of status is not likely to have the kind
of consequences which really motivate difficult or agonizing
reforms. The situation could resemble that of Britain today,
compared to what it once was.

'While competitively the British are not doing very well,
many Britons correctly say, "we never had it so good." And as
compared to their pre-World War II economic performance,
Britain indeed "never had it so good".' As a result there is no
particular social or political group in Britain which both has
sufficient power to cause radical change and frustration on a
scale as to want to bring about such change. As a result of their
loss in competitive status, many in Britain seem to indulge in a
kind of self-hatred, or assume a completely new and excessively

modest view of what Britain's role should be. Both of these attitudes are likely to be reproduced, if on a somewhat smaller scale, on the Continent.

'Moreover, it is now becoming increasingly recognized that the essence of the technological gap between Europe and the United States is less a question of markets and subsidies than of underlying factors *which seem to escape the political will of Europeans.*'

Such is the 'reasonable forecast' on which the Hudson Institute, as well as other institutions in the United States and Japan, have based their projections. When asked about the possibilities of a European change of attitude that might modify his predictions, Herman Kahn told us:

'The European Community, as we can envisage it, should be able to create and maintain an image of a well-functioning, multi-national, multi-lingual, multi-cultural entity which, despite this multiplicity of characteristics, has solved its really crucial problems. In addition, the community should appear as being of universal significance. Such a community could provide, in our opinion, an enormous sense of excitement and attraction for the aspirations of people both inside and outside of it and as a model to be emulated or supported. Its very internal diversity might make it particularly apt in dealing in an effective way with various nations in the underdeveloped world without overwhelming them. . . . While I previously indicated by scepticism that Europe will have a serious political community in the next decade or two, it still seems to me not wildly implausible that such a community could be organized.

'I think that if this occurred, it would conflict with very few nationalist or other European values, and enhance many. Such a community, if successful, would probably be the most important enterprise of the decade of the 1970's. Not only would it have a considerable direct influence, but it would be particularly important as a model for other nations to emulate, and might have an intensely beneficial effect on behaviour around the world as a force for order and justice. Because it could be clearly "equal" to the United States and the Soviet Union and superior to Japan before the end of this century, a European Political Community could cooperate with all of these on a much more satisfactory basis than the current Europe can. It is further likely to be under some pressure, both because of internal dynamics and because of competition with these other three powers, to produce important and spectacular projects for world order or world improvement. . . .

'From a strictly European point of view, the existence of such a community would remove from the Europeans any excuses that they lag behind because of inadequate size of enterprise, markets, or government subsidies. In ridding the Europeans of their complexes, it would permit them to concentrate their efforts on the social, cultural, and political factors which are much more serious than the purely technical problems, and are the very ones which in the final analysis will determine whether Europe can be competitive with the United States.'

There is no doubt that the problem is political. The technological, industrial, and financial formulas needed to raise European science and industry to the level of world competition are clear to any watchful observer of the process of modern growth. Political rigidity and self-defensive reflexes act as a brake on change, often dramatically so. Technological aptitude is not what is missing, but the will to change the rules of the social game. What our countries lack is political ambition. It is entirely up to us to provide it.

In examining the technological gap between Europe and the United States, Louis Armand also emphasizes mental attitudes over technological problems. Here are some of his comments on the material analysed in the first four parts of this book:

'How can Europe have an economic identity of her own? It would be a mistake to approach the problem only from this point of view, for this would ignore the elements that will enter into the problem during the years ahead. . . . If Europe is to play an important role, it is not enough to say that she must take part in global technological exchanges, however essential this may be. For Europe is to exist as a power, clearly the first condition is that she be economically united. But the second, and more difficult, condition is that she have a mentality of her own, an ethic, a political identity. This is where we are most retarded. . . . The absence of a uniquely European mode of thought is even clearer than the absence of a technological identity. That is what stands out the most.

'Europe ogles American wealth. Then, for conscience's sake,

and to compensate for her jealousy, she also stares at the under-developed countries—and this makes her cross-eyed. *Europe looks in two directions both in space and in time.* She looks back in time in the sense that she does not want to forget the glories of her empire or the satisfaction of her Commonwealth. It is hard for Europeans to forget their colonies, and that the language of diplomacy is French. Europe's gaze wanders be-tween East and West, between past and future. So long as she does not know what she wants, Europe has no chance of playing an important role in the emerging global civilization. ... But this necessary transformation of Europe is not going to happen spontaneously. *It needs strong-willed men who care about politics.*

'What counts in the end is not so much the equipment of a society, but its political-economic structure. The computer will unleash a far greater revolution than the assembly line. It will be adapted to everything, from law to the most elementary techniques. Europe still has a chance. She does not have to manufacture everything, but she must understand better than anyone else how to use the new technological equipment. This is a good deal more important.

'For every man who makes a machine (the computer), it takes ten men to think about ways of using it (software), and it will probably take a hundred to refine the programming of the soft-ware for one special technique or another. It is much harder to know how to use computers than how to make them. This is a question of intelligence and teamwork, and here lies Europe's chance if she can only understand the problem. *She must be more intelligent "structurally", since she has fallen so far behind in producing the equipment.* This is how Europe, if she can muster the political will, can stamp her own special seal on all aspects of tomorrow's world, from the social sciences to business management.'

Finally, a third confirmation of the problem was given by Jacques Maisonrouge. He doesn't talk politics; but when we asked him the reasons for Europe's lag, this is how he replied:

'What are the reasons for Europe's lag? We have to begin with our whole form of education. ... Aside from the training of children and the education of students, there is the important problem of creating a corps of trained personnel. European industrialists and businessmen have not yet understood that the training of managers is an absolute necessity.... Then there is the question of what can be called environment. European businessmen have a deep-seated need for security that expresses itself in old customs of market-sharing, cartels and business societies, agreements on common bidding, and price-fixing among firms in the same field. In the United States the atmosphere is different.... On the other hand, it cannot be doubted that in today's world, governments must exert an increasing control over economic life to stabilize the business cycle and prevent social crises in a system where the protection of the individual is of growing importance.... But European systems of education and administration exist in two separate worlds. On the one hand there is the world of industry that wants to "do business", and on the other hand the administrative world which is virtually ignorant of the real problems of business.... I am not saying that administrators are wrong and businessmen right; but it does seem that the economic effects of their professions are so different as to cause a real gap between them. This helps to maintain European class barriers—a hallmark of underdeveloped countries.... Finally European businessmen are reluctant to cooperate with union-management consultation committees and with trade union leaders.... *It is obvious that Europe's lag is not one of brain power, but of a lack of organization.*'

The American challenge forces us to face all our problems at once, and the least of these are technical. Above all, it is a matter of organizing production relations and social relations so that Europeans may fulfil the potential of their abilities and our industrial societies may acquire the capacity to fight back and win. It is a political problem.

The examples of Sweden and Japan, which we have already looked at, illustrate and prove that this is true. Europe has such a reservoir of talent and creative abilities that she can do more and do better. But with whom, on what can she build a new policy to meet this challenge?

We can go no further with reports by experts, statistical conclusions, and documentary evidence. At this point we have to shed our attempt at objectivity or neutrality, and plunge ahead.

The success of other countries suggests that the *fundamental condition* for an industrial society to catch up is a high level of social integration—a kind of peaceful stability, or at least an absence of civil war, that will allow the society to concentrate on the mechanics of change. In particular this involves:

—the value placed on individual and social security in a time of technological development.

—the generally-accepted importance of government leadership.

—a decision by the whole population to do what must be done to build a truly independent society.

We Europeans have to take all these factors into account if we hope to escape the alienation that give birth to communism. We have to rely on the values and political forces that preserve Europe's special quality, and which are most likely to promote the adaptations necessary for growth. Otherwise there could be a legitimate revolt by those elements of the society most threatened by change.

This may be a debatable interpretation—especially since it underlines the continuing importance of traditional ideas that are linked with social democracy in Germany and Scandinavia, with the Labour party in Britain, and with the Left in Latin countries. We will limit ourselves to what is a personal interpretation, the interpretation of a man in the forty-year-old generation for whom the American challenge is the crucial question, one we cannot appeal. If the generation now assuming positions of power, and determining the direction our societies will take is unable to meet this challenge, it will never have a second chance. The Europe we will pass on in 1980 to men who today are twenty years old will be a continent outside the mainstream of history, leading a life without vitality or purpose, under the shadow of its dependence on America.

The interpretation and the commitment of a Frenchman persuaded, from a study of the material objectivity presented here, that social integration and European recovery go hand-in-hand with a *new demand for justice* and with bringing up-to-date the old values of *confidence in man*, which are the natural heritage of what has been known historically as the Left. These are values, moreover, which have been applied in the development of the United States itself through the influence and action of the liberal wing of the Democratic Party.

The fate of Europe and the fate of the Left are linked together by the American challenge. If the Left, particularly in France, remains what it has been, the chances for social integration—the key to change—will be nil, and so will chances for Europe to raise her technological power up to the level of world competition.

Even if there is no real chance for social integration, technological evolution and international competition will impose change. But it will come painfully, provoking friction, jolts, and resistance.

If, however, the Left can overcome its instinctive reflexes of nervousness and fear when faced with the mounting tempo of progress, and can rediscover the traditional values for which it stands, it can liberate so much energy in France and throughout Europe that all the elements in the equation can be changed. Salvation can come only through such an awakening.

The word 'Left', with all that it implies, is not being used in this book from sectarianism, nostalgia for the past, or a mania for classifications. It would be foolish to write off as profits and losses the intellectual, emotional, and historical capital of the Left at the very moment when it can help the cause of European development. The Left must put an end to the internecine conflicts and divisions that hold back French society. Solving them would be a real contribution to European recovery.

A country like France cannot achieve the degree of organization and efficiency it needs to play a key role in building the European community and replying to the American challenge so long as the various participants in the political, economic, and social game continue to contradict and ignore each other. So long as management persists in opposing labour, and labour refuses to cooperate with management, so long as the government denies the legitimacy of the opposition and the opposition that of the government, none of the necessary changes can take place. The rifts in French society will continue to cause terrible waste and to weaken Europe.

The Left is often accused of pursuing fantasies: general disarmament, abolition of class barriers, world government, etc.

Here, for once, is a project which might achieve these goals. If it doesn't make the attempt, the Left will lose its *raison d'être*, which is to rally all men—not just the elite—to take the future into their hands. In a satellite Europe, plans for the democratization of education, knowledge, and business would become ludicrous, and debates on the meaning of democracy would be meaningless. We no longer have to ask whether Western Europe should choose the path of Soviet bureaucratization. Our only choice is whether we want to be a poor imitation of the United States, or seek our triumphs by following our own special genius. Some of the things that are particularly European—efforts to go beyond the rationale of the market economy, the collectivization of risk, and limitations on the role of money—are in large part the contribution of the Left. The prospects for an independent Europe and for a revitalized Left are, as we shall see, intimately linked.

In 1936 the reformer who had been elected President of the United States, confronted with the gravest economic and social crisis his country had ever known, made his famous statement: 'This generation of Americans has a rendezvous with destiny.' These Americans assumed their responsibilities, and by a sudden burst of support for the New Deal, launched the United States on the path of power at the very moment when she seemed to have lost all ambition.

This generation of Europeans, nearly half a century later, also has a rendezvous with destiny.

CHAPTER 22

THE PROGRESSIVE FORCE

THE give and take, the dialectic, between a moderate party and a liberal party are as essential to economic growth as to democracy. Social progress and democracy can never be by-products of technological innovation, even when, as today, technology opens up vast new perspectives in which they can operate. *Politics, the interplay between Right and Left, is increasingly the irreplaceable source of creativity.*

The French Left, like France herself, is at the heart of the European problem. If France does not play her role, then everything will become atrophied and sterile. What went wrong with the Left? Can it ever recover its integrity and its mission? These questions are important to Frenchmen who do not belong to the Left, just as they are to Europeans who are not French.

The Left carries within itself a contradiction—one that gives it much of its value, and at the same time is the source of its troubles. While the Right follows the tides of history with its ups and downs, the Left, by its very nature, is split between opposition and responsibility. It must refuse to accept society as it is, but it cannot repudiate society altogether. It wants to build utopias and draw from them the strength to overcome seemingly insuperable obstacles. It must set its sights on distant goals which will guide its actions from day to day. It wants to keep its distance from a present it finds dissatisfying, but must, nonetheless, always be capable of dealing with this if.

There was a time when the prospect of revolution simplified matters. Lenin could ignore the whole process of industrialization and the liberalization of the Tsarist Empire because he

152

planned to get rid of it and replace it with an entirely new order. The Bolsheviks operated within the framework of the bourgeois world only to denounce it, dissolve it, and destroy it.

For the same reason, communists think they can behave, or at least speak as though it were possible to do everything at once: raise wages, cut working hours, lower taxes, and increase government spending. The misunderstanding that separates them from their neighbours on the traditional Left comes from the fact that they start from different hypotheses. By the nature of its thought, the revolutionary Left lives in the future, or even in dreams—as does the Right today. From the moment that revolution becomes impractical or inopportune—as it is in highly industrialized countries—and where it appears obvious that it would force Europe into isolation and stagnation, the task of the Left becomes more complicated.

It must live simultaneously in 1968 and 1988, commute between reality and utopia. So long as the Left maintains a balance between the demands of its ideals and the limitations of the present, the tension between these two forces gives it dynamism. This is the operating principle of Swedish socialists, who every year keep improving society they have been managing for forty years.

When this dialectic dies out, the Left becomes more conservative, either through impotence or conformity. Whether it loses sight of its origins or of its objectives, the result is the same; it ceases to be a force for change. The Left has lost its balance by being so contentious. Its justified criticism of capitalism has degenerated into a cult of bureaucracy, and its criticism of authoritarianism into an apology for political weakness. Its messianic attitude has alienated it from the world we live in and the problems we must deal with.

The criticism of capitalism was more than justified by its injustices and its inadequate production. The Left, backed up by the lessons of periodic recessions, naturally should have tried to strengthen the central government and establish authority over the economy by the only means then known to it—nationalization.

But in this day-by-day battle, a kind of transference took place. Everything that was private—private enterprise, private property, private initiative—was thought to be Evil, while everything that was public was identified with the Good. Despite reservations in socialist thought about bureaucracy and the bourgeois state, every time some area of the economy attracted their attention or got into trouble, socialists got into the habit of demanding nationalization or restricting competition by heavy taxation and restrictive quotas.

Only a small minority interested itself in new methods that could eventually correct the abuses and gaps of the market economy without destroying its incentives and responsiveness. Nationalization has remained a kind of all-purpose 'Open Sesame' for the Left. The result has been a double confusion— between property and power, between economic planning and bureaucracy.

Power is no longer linked to property. This is demonstrated by large corporations which control key areas of production. Everyone knows that the rights of stockholders are now limited to cashing in coupons, and the board of directors to ratifying decisions made by management.

In his book *The New Industrial State*, economist John Kenneth Galbraith, who has sparked new ideas on the American Left, has outlined the new situation:

'This shift of power has been disguised because, as was once true of land, the position of capital is imagined to be immutable. That power should be elsewhere seems unnatural and those who so argue seem to be in search of frivolous novelty. And it has been disguised because power has not gone to another of the established factors as they are celebrated in conventional economic pedagogy. It has not passed to labour. Labour has won limited authority over its pay and working conditions but none over the enterprise. . . .

'Nor has power passed to the classical entrepreneur—the individual who once used his access to capital to bring it into combination with the other factors of production. He is a diminishing figure in the industrial system. . . .

'Power has, in fact, passed to what anyone in search of novelty might be justified in calling a new factor of production. This is the association of men of diverse technical knowledge, experience or other talent which modern industrial technology and planning require. . . . It is on the effectiveness of this organization, as most business doctrine now implicitly agrees,

that the success of the modern business enterprise now depends.
Were this organization dismembered or otherwise lost, there is
no certainty that it could be put together again. To enlarge it to
undertake new tasks is an expensive and sometimes uncertain
undertaking. . . .'[1]

This is confirmed by the experience of numerous firms,
particularly by the great commercial banks, whose methods
remained virtually unchanged after they were taken over by
the State. But belief in the miracles of nationalization has made
many on the Left forget where they want to go and has spared
them the trouble of figuring out how to get there. Since the Left
views the State as a fortress from which great armies would one
day set forth to conquer the enemy, practical methods for
establishing 'popular sovereignty' over the economic terrain, or
at least improving conditions without civil war, have not
aroused a great deal of interest.

The Soviet model held an obvious fascination for those who
have understood that this is precisely the purpose of long-range
economic planning. For a long time a large section of the
communist Left, and even non-communists saw the shape of
the future in a system conceived in 1928 for a society with
despotic traditions and a retarded economy—and even badly
adapted to the level of maturity later achieved by the Soviet
Union itself. What the State lacked was the internal coherence
and resolution to provide a framework for coordinated action
of autonomous units (public and private), by a *strategy of
development*.

The first condition of this coherence—authority and the
stability of executive power—was rejected by the traditional
Left. Although government interventions were sacrosanct, the
State itself was suspect.

Criticism of authoritarianism in a country like France, which
is steeped in it to the point of sickness, was as justified as the
criticism of capitalism. But there, too, this criticism missed the
target. There was a battle to be waged to make democracy something concrete, real, and ordinary, in business as in the provinces; in the cities as in the political parties; in government
economic planning as in the administration of our educational
system, or in the rules governing radio and television. But the

[1] Boston: Houghton Mifflin (1967), pp. 58–59.

Left usually preferred to fight against a powerful executive—
without which it is impossible to control economic forces—and
also to fight against 'technocracy', which is nonetheless a useful
instrument for achieving this ambition, provided there is a
strong government to manage it.

A love for bureaucratic solutions and a taste for a weak
executive are seemingly contradictory. But the two together
have helped to reduce the role of freedom and human will in the
management of our society. The former favoured the reduction
of competition, initiative, and risk—which our bourgeois
dynasties were only too happy to see happen. The taste for a
weak executive has prevented the State from giving our social
and economic system the degree of efficiency and equity it could
have had if government interventions had been better planned
and less disjointed.

But what has most weakened the Left is the apparent reversal
of its reflexes regarding the future. 'Those who feared the
future now adapt to it, for they see it as a reassuring extension
of the present; those who lived for the future have lost the keys
to it and are groping in the dark; they dread its dangers and
seek refuge in their traditions.' The author of this statement, the
French sociologist Edgar Morin, cites the case of a rural community in Finistère.

Prewar reactionaries, the representatives of the most prominent conservative families, have all changed; they accept the
present, and even the future, with confidence. Socialist leaders
of the community, on the other hand, are consumed by anguish
when they contemplate the future. Not only are modern forms
of leisure and the tastes of young people abhorrent to them, but
the future itself is a source of anguish. 'We don't know where
we're going anymore,' or 'We've lost our way in the dark'—
such phrases naturally come to their minds when they look
toward the horizon.

For the right-wing French theoretician, Charles Maurras, the
Golden Age was considered to be something long since gone by
—the classical order, the nearly miraculous product of the meeting between Greek thought and Catholicism. Any innovation
threatened to upset this balance of enduring harmony.

The *petite peur* of the twentieth century was rooted in the
hard core of the Right, which sometimes saw the future as a

democratic ant-heap, and sometimes in the form of a world enslaved by robots. This attitude is now dying out. The Vatican Council has encouraged the birth of a new spirit in the Catholic church, where in France there is only a small reactionary element. As for those on the modern political Right today, the future seems to lie with America—a thought in which they take comfort.

The Left has several Golden Ages, the last being the Popular Front in 1936. It had its limits, as Roger Priouret has observed: 'Leon Blum governed for only ten months and was overwhelmed by the problems of the factories even before he came to power. He could not apply devaluation with a cool head, nor could he refuse the 40-hour week which undermined economic expansion. The year 1936 marked an explosion of the working class after a long and terrible crisis, just as there was an explosion in 1945 after the suffering of the Occupation. The least we can hope for in the future is that such events will not take place again.'

But myths are often more tenacious than facts, and the Paradise Lost of the Left glitters even more brightly than the Promised Land that has not yet been glimpsed. On the far Left there is even, as Edgar Morin has written, 'the fear of a barbarous future where television, dance halls, selfishness, and sensuality would sweep away the fruits of centuries of humanism.'

It could be said, in short, that a rapid evolution on the Right has led it to take over positions once held by the Left—sports-loving politicians, dynamic engineers, and technocrats trained to think that the future lies with them. Would not the Right once again, this time for different reasons—be better able to govern in the context of change brought about by permanent technological innovation?

During the time when good management was identified with monetary stability, the Right had the upper hand. Now that an effective government must urge continual adaptation to change, doesn't the Right still have the trumps? When the Left in the 1930's promised brighter tomorrows, many 'ordinary people' feared that by voting for it they would see utopianism flourish in the government. Now that the electorate has developed a taste for the future and a desire for progress which ought normally to bring the Left to power, does it still have these qualities?

Too simple a reply would ignore an important bit of evidence: the cultural characteristics which explain both European adaptation and resistance to change are in large part shared by the Right and the Left. They form what can, without exaggeration, be called the national temperament. Two factors, however, have operated in favour of the Right:

—a powerful explosive has become a soporific;

—power renews itself, rather than wearing away.

The Left once had a powerful explosive in its hands—revolution. This is the explosive that has turned into a soporific. 'I do not now see any powerful explosives,' writes François Bloch-Lainé. 'I wish that those on the Left, who borrow the dialectic of communists but stop short of their conclusion, would explain exactly what they want to happen, what kind of socialism would be born from the destruction of our present economic structure. There were new forces in France in 1788 and in Russia in 1916 oppressed by the privileged and ready to take over from an abusive and decadent power. Is this true in France today, and is it so widespread that the majority of the population can be made happier only by overthrowing the whole system? Who and what would survive from such an upheaval, except a Soviet-style dictatorship?'

New forces, which were trapped in the Russia of 1916 by corrupt leadership, are captives in today's France of what remains of a revolutionary ideology. In the beginning this ideology was motivated by something positive. The present was so insupportable that only a revolution could break through into the future. Imperceptibly the meaning of this proposition has been reversed for the old militants: the hope for a brighter tomorrow is so comforting that it does away with the need to change the present.

We have seen a hundred times how the more and more theoretical perspective of an increasingly distant upheaval has served as an alibi for the conservatism of political machines. But the hope that a new world will somehow come about also makes it easier for those at the bottom of the social ladder. The American sociologist Jesse Pitts has observed that in contemporary France this hope plays a role analogous to that attributed by Marx to religion in nineteenth-century capitalism. Inspired by the conviction that they will be on the top in the better world to come, those on the bottom are better able to endure the injustices of the present. The vision of the Promised Land disarms the warriors. For militants its annunciation eliminates the need for actions which might bring it into being.

Unfortunately this parallel is not meant to be amusing. An enormous part of the courage and devotion of labour leaders is spent on ideological demands which spare management the concrete concessions that a more aggressive policy could obtain. In order to keep up their radical credentials, these leaders make the greatest possible number of extreme demands without bothering to find out whether or not the firm can grant them. Nothing is easier for management than to squash a strike, or choose from the list of grievances those whose satisfaction will trouble it the least. These, of course, are not the ones which are most important to the workers.

This tendency to be diverted by decoys has made the Left lose a good many battles it should have won. The traditional Left has never stopped behaving as though it were still in the situation of the Communards of 1871, encircled by the Versailles government army ready to wipe it out. Jules Vallès, one of the French writers of the period, described the situation in these words: 'The important thing is to explain what we would like, since we cannot do what we want. This was said by one of the Commune cabinet ministers in drawing up his programme for a government that was soon to be crushed by the Versailles army.

Demanding the impossible or the unnecessary, the Left has neglected to attack where it might have had a chance of success. But today its encirclement is imaginary. It is due for the most part to what is left of the old messianism. This messianism separates the 'pure' Communist Party from the rest of the Left, which is 'less pure'. For many people socialism is considered to be a milder version of communism—communism minus concessions to democratic legality and the bourgeois order. The definition by subtraction still prevents the non-communist Left from being morally sure of itself, and assert itself fully, calmly, and with a sense of legitimacy as the true Left.

How many people on the Left cannot help glancing over their shoulder to make sure that the Communist Party, that moral censor, is not looking at them too critically, or to prove to themselves that they are even more faithful than the Party? With the revolutionary myth pulling from one side and necessity from the other, language becomes twisted and confused.

The left-wing intellectual is split between thesis and hypothesis—the thesis being that all means of production must be socialized; the hypothesis being that it is better not to do anything because it would destroy the resiliency of the economy. Sometimes the Left delves into the logic of management reform; sometimes it calls for final answers and demands the 'urgent nationalization of banks, iron and steel mills, oil, atomic energy, shipyards, and the chemical industry.' This confusion over means and ends, this unintentional deceit, these doubts about its own legitimacy, contribute greatly to reducing the progressive force of the Left and preventing it from really becoming a 'go-ahead' party.

A second factor that disturbs the Left's attitude towards the future and favours the awakening and revitalization of the Right is that power renews itself, while the strength of those in the opposition wears away.

The traditional belief is that the exercise of power gradually undermines the popularity of officials, exhausts men and ideas, and finally leads to the almost automatic return of the opposition to power. This view of things is no longer so true. Conservatives elected to power have usually taken advantage of it to modernize their party structure, find capable young men, and change their attitude towards critical problems. Why?

All professions today recognize the continual development of new knowledge and skills as an absolute necessity. Politics does not escape this rule, and indeed escapes it least of all, because it is the most difficult of all professions. A good politician must keep abreast of a great many facts, maintain contact with an enormous number of people in the most diverse areas, master, or at least be able to manage, a variety of techniques—or else lose his qualifications for his job. But these people, facts, and techniques change along with everything else, and just as fast. Those in positions of power enjoy a remarkable means for continuous training that those in the opposition are denied. The entire government machinery of information, analysis, and forecasting is at their disposition. Even if they do not shed their dogmas, this machinery allows them to maintain contact with the increasingly complex and fast-moving realities they work with. While some, of course, do not know how to profit from it, a great many others continue to improve their capacities.

Despite his remarkable ability for assimilating new material, the new French chief of state was still in a pre-economic stage of political analysis in 1958. On returning to power that year, General de Gaulle discovered the advantages of the Common Market and the Plan. His sense of 'ardent duty' even led him to glimpse the epic dimensions of his own administration. Government officials live in symbiosis with the technocracy. While this technocracy has its faults, it was, after all, the Inspecteurs des Finances and the graduates of the Ecole Polytechnique who after the war developed such important French institutions as the Plan, the Commission for National Accounts, and the Prevision, economic forecasts drawn up by the National Planning Commissariat. This gave the French economy a much-needed method of planning for the future, one which had not occurred to prewar politicians (the Popular Front never mentioned the Plan). It was the technocracy that the ideology of growth took form.

The continuous exercise of governmental responsibility—not the use of documents as textbooks and technicians as tutors—has forced conservatives to change. However respectful they may be of inherited attitudes, it is difficult to survive for very long in a position of leadership in an advanced country without taking action—or of acting without taking account of the realities of a world in constant movement.

Economic laws are cited to force the Left to recognize that it would follow similar policies if it were in power. The Left, we should remember, operates under the same restraints as its adversaries. Conditioned by his responsibilities as French prime minister, George Pompidou is led to support a Fifth Economic Plan which no one with a sense of reality could call reactionary. Similarly, once Harold Wilson came to power he was, for lack of another way of resolving Britain's persistent economic crises, converted to pushing for the admission of Britain into the Common Market. Power stimulates the digestion of new ideas—and necessity forces those in power to consume them. Thus moderates have borrowed as heavily from ideas put into circulation these last few years by the Left as have left-wing groups themselves. At one time they use them for action, at another time only for the sake of employing a modern vocabulary. But that doesn't matter, for the ideas change them.

Conversely, a large part of the Left has grown anaemic from being too long in the opposition. By remaining outside the political game for a long time in a country that changes so fast, a party risks losing contact with reality. If it is not in daily contact with these realities it is tempted to apply the same old analyses and to live with outdated ideas. Social-Democrats in neighbouring countries have seen the danger of 'eternal rest', and have understood that instead of growing fat in the pastures of the opposition, they would more likely become sickly and dull.

In 1963 Pietro Nenni, the old Marxist militant who was tied to the Italian Communist Party by years of common struggle, launched an 'opening to the Left' so that his party could re-enter the circle of power. In 1963 and 1964 Harold Wilson tenaciously fought two electoral battles to seize and consolidate power. In 1966 the chiefs of the German Social-Democratic party agreed, in opposition to party traditionalists, to form a coalition government with the conservatives. They succeeded against the wishes of the old militants who believed, as always, that a little more patience would bring the Social-Democrats a greater, if more distant, victory.

These three efforts to return to power could be called survival operations undertaken to escape from a debilitating numbness. The French left-wing parties, for their part, suffer even more from their exclusion from power because the French parliament does not include the opposition in the work of the majority, and neither the parties nor the National Assembly possesses the power it should have.

It is not easy for a French parliamentarian—harassed by the problems of his constituency, split between Paris and his district in the provinces, and condemned to political tinkering—to maintaining truly professional qualifications. Inadequately informed, deprived of expert opinion and research services, too long shut off from political responsibility, the Left as a whole tends to fuss over old problems rather than regenerate itself. This is why it faces the terrible temptation of sliding from the political minority, to being against power in general; and from being anti-power, to becoming anti-society.

The opposition criticizes the government—that is its duty and its job. But two tactics are open to it: say what it would do differently if it were in power; or continually, and on general principle, oppose every decision of the government. By adopting this second tactic without reservation and exploiting to the full the short-run possibilities it offers, the opposition is necessarily driven to condemn not only the government's mistakes, but the things it does well; criticize not only its deliberate acts, but hold it responsible for dangers that occur inevitably and independent of its desires. It will protest against unemployment in the coal mines and against the flight from the farms. It will defy forces of change even if they help, whatever their abuses, to give the country a new look. Technocrats, big business, and dynamic men are equally suspect to such an opposition.

If this is carried to an extreme, the opposition could succumb to the *petite peur* of the twentieth century and fret about the development of television or the use of computers. In the beginning the target was the government; in the end it risks being change itself. The opposition could become the political expression of an 'anti-society' mentality.

It is proper that the Left should espouse the cause of the 'victims of development', those who cannot keep pace with growth, often because society is so badly organized. More than ever they need skillful advocates and efficient representatives. Since wealth attracts wealth, it is too easy to forget and sacrifice these victims. But it is not always their fate that the opposition concerns itself with; often it is their protests in their crudest form.

Georges Lavau has well summarized the 'working-class-protest-election' language of the Communist Party, which in reality forms a kind of stock-in-trade of the traditional Left: 'More government spending, a vast housing programme, reduction of taxes for the poor and the middle class.' This confused programme is more than simply a vulgar poujadism,[2] and Lavau is quite right in observing: 'Aside from the obvious, there are good reasons for the Communist Party to refuse to adopt the vocabulary of the government in power. In the context of

[2] A reference to Pierre Poujade, a right-wing politician whose nationalistic, demagogic appeal to peasants and low-income groups made a considerable impact on French politics in the 1950's.

today's France it can establish its identity only in terms of a struggle with established governments and by promising eventually to overthrow them. It remains a prisoner of the devastating critique Marx made of the ideology of the State. Considering itself the historic agent of the working class, it remains closely tied to the instincts and the experience of this class, which in France is unsympathetic to government and often anti-authority. It instinctively feels that, until it is able to assume power, any logically consistent programme stands in its way and hobbles its movements.'

The revolutionary and anarchist-trade union traditions of the Left are intensified in their effects by a peculiar disease of the opposition in times of rapid change—remoteness from reality and from responsibilities that in the long-run breed distaste for them.

It is even fair to ask whether the refusal to come to terms not only with capitalism, but with the world as it is, may not be one of the reasons for the stability and prestige of the Communist Party. Since the end of the war the French standard of living has doubled, the life of the average Frenchman has been profoundly changed, and Moscow has ceased to be the beacon of the world revolution. Yet despite all predictions of the decline of the French Communist Party, it attracts as many votes as ever.

Even more, despite Budapest, the shift from Stalinism to de-Stalinization, and a hundred tactical policy switches, many on the Left continue to see the Communist Party as a beacon of morality in politics. An alliance with the Party is pure; the other parties are tainted. Why? Certainly the Communist Party has many working-class members, but it has no monopoly on the disadvantaged. A public opinion poll reveals that, on the whole, those who vote Communist are no poorer than those who vote for other parties. Perhaps the source of its prestige lies in its monopoly on the refusal to compromise. No compromise with power, no compromise with capitalist society in general. This 'purity' has an undeniable appeal.

The possibility of a Left-wing government is made much less credible by this exaggerated negativism. It also deprives the Left of votes it might normally win. If the Left is against so many things—technocrats, executive power, big business, profits—it is hard to see exactly what its objectives are, despite recent efforts to clarify them. Does it want to do away with the market economy or improve it? Stay forever in opposition or perpetually in the government? Accept or reject the democratic game, which means alternating in power with the opposition, and peaceful relations between majority and minority? Return to rule by the National Assembly or maintain a strong executive? The vagueness of its aims leaves an impression of insecurity, confusion, and deviousness.

If it is to recapture a coherent strategy so crucial in the industrial era, the Left must go all the way in the revisionism that it has already begun in France and the other European countries, and which is helping it to regain its identity. There is something, however, that holds its leaders back, and prevents them from accepting these changes. The Left fears it may fade away if it repudiates those symbols which it finds increasingly hard to believe in itself. Without its revolutionary messianism, its hostility to the temporal power of the Church, and its nostalgia for parliamentarianism, what would it have left to call its own?

Everything—its objectives and its motives. For the Left to outlive its usefulness, one of two things must happen: it must win its objectives or find they are totally unattainable, or else there must be such unanimity about these objectives that there is no longer a conservative opposition for the Left to combat. Now is the time when the very things that socialism has promised to man have ceased to be a dream, thanks to developments in science, technology, and modern methods of work.

One of the oldest ambitions of socialism has been to provide every working man with an interesting job. This ambition may soon become possible, since automation will do away with mechanical tasks and piece-work, and allow everyone to become a skilled worker. It is not important that the road we have travelled is not the one foreseen by the doctrinaire socialists of the last century. The originality of the Left, its very *raison d'être*, lies in the objectives that it seeks, not in the methods for attaining them, which are always subject to change.

There is no guarantee that everything will turn out for the best. While Europe is wealthier today than at any moment in her history, inequalities of income have increased over the past ten years. Uncontrolled economic development strengthens the strong and weakens the weak. It makes snowballs of wealth that leave behind inexcusable pockets of misery, even in the richest country in the world.

Unless we apply a principle of equity, the tremendous economic expansion of the last decades of this century could give birth to a savage society of man against man. Those on the Left must look towards the future where they will see the outlines of their mission, a mission of fidelity not to tradition, but to inspiration and to rational goals.

The basic values of the Left are, as we will try to show, invaluable sources of strength and effectiveness in the struggle to meet the American challenge. By freeing itself from fortuitous corruptions of its values, the Left can recapture its identity and its competence to once again become an indispensable progressive force.

PART 6

THE WELLSPRINGS OF POWER

CHAPTER 23

GROWTH AND JUSTICE

PROFESSOR SALAZAR'S techniques of 'good management', which broke all European records for monetary stability, illiteracy, and economic stagnation, were the envy of conservatives all over the Continent before the last war. They admired the vigorous economic liberalism applied by the Portuguese premier's economic adviser, Jacques Rueff, and confirmed by the good standing of the escudo. A sound currency, security of investments, order in the streets—these criteria of success expressed the wisdom of a paralysed society.

Such criteria left little hope for those who were victims of the real disorder that lay behind the façade of 'good management'. Newspapers today still regularly receive letters praising the pre-war era. Yet recent studies have shown that between the two wars, production in France fell by 20 per cent.

If this context social justice seemed an act of subversion, and any effort to reduce inequalities appeared to be a punitive expedition against the ruling class.

Power was a trap for the Left. If it observed the rules of the game, it had to respect the status quo, and thus betray itself; if it rejected these rules, it faced failure. The stock market fell, capital fled the country, and prices rose. One part of the economic equation was missing: growth. The appearance of this factor and the pre-eminent place it has taken in the calculations of experts and in the public consciousness have completely changed our perspective.

From now on, good management can be measured. The annual growth rate of the economy provides a gauge of full employment. 'The need to stay above the 4-per-cent annual

169

growth rate has become a political imperative. It has the virtue of simplicity and the hitherto unknown advantage in the political world of being measurable. Below 4 per cent is failure, above is success.'[1]

We know that continued expansion is not possible without stability, since inflation undermines the fundamental equilibrium of prices, foreign trade, and investment. The new criterion embraces the old, condemning stagnation and respect for eternal order on which the doctrine of conservatism is based.

The choice of a new standard of good management obliges those on the Left, as well as those on the Right, to revise their thinking. It forces the former to take a hard look at the mechanism of production, and the latter to adapt to a dynamism foreign to their way of thinking. Both have had to recognize that *rapid and lasting economic growth is the point of departure for any policy*, domestic or foreign.

Obviously it is not an end in itself. Like any creed obsessively dedicated to its own methods (whether they be free enterprise or the Plan, monetary stability or expansion), the religion of growth leads to the neglect of men and their needs. It is equally certain that the degree of autonomy, prosperity, and social justice—and these three are linked together—that a country aspires to depend upon its growth rate. A society enjoying rapid growth is free to define its own form of civilization because it can establish its order of priorities. A stagnant society cannot really exercise the right of self-determination.

In an expanding society the political debate is framed in these terms: 'Should we join the space race or step up aid to the underdeveloped countries of the "third world"? Beautify our cities or exploit the sea floor? Develop nuclear energy or build more automobiles?' In a stagnant society acquired attitudes and, above all, restraints from the outside determine policy.

The corollary of growth is *change*. To grow richer, as they have done, although too slowly, for the past twenty years, the French have had to wrench themselves loose with great difficulty from many habits that were dear to them. There can be no progress without surrendering acquired privileges, without discarding outdated machinery, ideas, and skills. The crisis in

[1] *La Politique des Revenus* by Jean Boissonnat.

management affecting the 40-year-olds stems from a conflict between a frozen educational system and constantly changing administrative techniques. This unsettling change is quite different from a general upheaval. It is neither a succession of storms and lulls, nor a staccato revolution, but a *continuous adjustment*.

Change is the very essence of growth—less addition than it is substitution, less accumulation than transformation. Projects are born, grow, reach their peak, decline, and die in the fervour of creative destruction described by Schumpeter and discussed by Pierre Massé:

'The basis for rapid expansion is a continual redistribution of work and capital assuring their application to the most productive ends at all times. This mobilization of resources which everyone recommends implies a mobility many refuse. It is no longer enough to agree to isolated changes, separated by long slack periods. We must learn to live in the midst of accelerating change. This state of constant receptivity, this need to "stay looser", is a kind of "shock" to many. Change can be deeply unsettling to those who have to give up their job, their home, their friends, and their habits. But even if a man stays in the same place, things change around him. There are too many outdated ideas, unnecessary jobs, obsolete techniques, and shabby cities. At the same time, there are too many new ideas, untried jobs, undeveloped techniques, and cities without roots.'[2]

The new forms of progress bear no resemblance to the old ones; and particularly not to the necessary, but brutal, wave of reforms that followed the last war—sweeping nationalizations, adoption of Social Security, sudden modernization of basic industries. A quick, steady pace is now replacing the old jerky leaps.

A permanent state of change is overturning all our theoretical ideas about the art of government. Conservation of what is outdated and old ideas of 'good management' necessarily become bad economics. A government that does not continually try to adapt its use of men and economic structures is a bad manager, just as an engineer who gets by on what he learned as a student is a bad technician.

The 'good old wisdom' of conservatives, the cardinal virtue

[2] Pierre Massé, *Le Plan ou l'Anti-Hasard*.

of traditional management, no longer serves to 'maintain stability'; on the contrary, it causes insecurity, crises, and suffering.

There is no shortage of everyday examples—miners made prisoners of their condemned mine, teachers overwhelmed by crowded classes, unlivable cities, undrivable roads, and unworkable telephones. All these are due to narrow vision and slow reflexes. There is no point here in holding a tiresome trial of the Fourth and Fifth Republics, for they are equally responsible—or rather it is the French community as a whole that has not yet understood the consequences of the rapid change it is undergoing.

It is easy to say, now that they have occurred, that many of these things could have been avoided. But to diagnose what must be done today to spare the Europeans of 1980 other maladies whose germs are already infecting us is a good deal harder and requires coordinated teamwork. Despite the vogue for growth, we still have a static image of government. The agitation for reform that rages in several fields, particularly education, offers only a faint semblance of adjustment to change. It reveals the nervousness of ossified institutions when faced with an evolution too rapid for them to handle.

In the traditional view, 'phases of management' alternate with 'phases of reform'. It can even be said, and the idea is widespread, that the Right takes care of the former and the Left the latter. The Left reforms, and squanders. The Right digests, and accumulates. Raymond Poincaré built up the reserves, Léon Blum dispensed gifts. Peaceful periods are punctuated by crises, which correct injustices by using the profits from the preceding phase. This interpretation, however, has never fitted the facts, and cannot stand up to historical analysis. Today it is clear that the principle itself is false: he who refuses to change wastes his resources.

By a kind of irony, at the very moment that the quickening pace of change is overturning the old criteria of 'good management', the traditional positions of Right and Left seem to have been reversed, and the Left once more is in a bad condition for taking up the reins of power. Nonetheless the Left has enormous reserve capacity for progress that the Right does not have, and could not have. Conservatives have certainly shown their technical skills, but have not accepted the full consequences of expansion. They have not profited enough from their skills to attack the roots of underdevelopment in France.

Taking France as an example, if we look at her basic institutions, we perceive that the essential features of an unusually authoritarian and continuous regime have scarcely changed. Such brilliant short-term manœuvres as the devaluation of 1958, or the stabilization of 1963, stand out against a background of myopia. Easily predictable crises, like the one in Social Security or in the dying industries, have ripened for years without our leaders bothering about them. Tactics have been better than strategy. But *the faster the movement, the more strategy counts.*

In 1959 there were two major areas of decay: our industrial structure and our financial system. Within a few years the Common Market and the Kennedy Round will expose French industry to the full force of international competition. Yet unless it goes through some far-reaching changes, industry will not be able to keep up with this competition. Its financial structure and its capacity for technological innovation are inadequate. Most of the large corporations are weaker than not only the American giants, but German and Dutch firms as well. There are no areas where French industry outclasses its rivals. In order to adapt, it has to concentrate, specialize, and cut away fat.

Although this has to be done quickly at the European level, it does not mean that we cannot start in France. The remodelling of institutions that have grown up and grown old in the shadow of protection will disrupt personal lives and professional habits—and may exceed the capacities of business to control. The government must take the initiative. If, for example, something has to be done to combine the forces of the three major firms in the electronics industry, it is up to the government to do it. Regardless of their rivalries, business executives cannot turn down a government that is their biggest customer and controls their credit. But our officials will not interfere, for it is against tradition for the State to become so involved in private business.[3]

[3] There are some interesting exceptions, such as Pechiney-Trefimeteaux, or Ugine-Kuhlman, and later the *plan-calcul* for electronics, whose limitations we tried to show.

Since 1954 France has had a modern system of indirect taxation through the TVA (tax on added value, calculated at each stage from production to sale), but its system of direct taxation has been falling to pieces. The tax schedule applies only to salaried employees. In other categories the tax is adjusted to take account of fraud, and fraud is justified by the severity of the tax rate. A tax base designed to aid the small farmer provides the big landowner with a large income. In industry, commerce, and the professions, the relationship between income and taxes is purely imaginary, for the real rates vary according to the business and the individual. Thousands of subsidies and penalties are distributed by chance.

Double-dealing is widespread, and almost obligatory. In 1963, 85 per cent of the farm population was considered to have earned less than 1,410 francs a year—and thus did not have to pay taxes. One third of French business firms declared a deficit. Between 3 and 4 billion francs in 'general expenses' went into the paychecks of executives. These figures, which the Finance Ministry knows better than anyone, have not persuaded it to find a more equitable tax system.

Such are the limits of conservative good management. Can we go beyond them? Economists—not from left-wing sentiments but from realism—attach a growing importance to the human factors involved in expansion: the quality of management, ability of the workers to assimilate new techniques, group support of objectives, and agreement among various elements of society on the rules of the industrial game. While these factors have nothing to do with mechanics, they enter into the calculations of economists and now take first place—the same place where unrepentant 'capitalism' reigns. It is in these areas that economists seek the reason for disparities in the rate of growth in technologically advanced countries. The most forward-looking elements in management, the labour unions, and the technocracy are now concentrating on one of these elements— *the degree of integration of wage earners in a system no longer based on stability, but on growth.*

Before the war, wage earners represented 45 per cent of the active population; today more than 75 per cent. They are by far the strongest single group in number, buying power, and savings. Yet the majority of this majority continues to think and behave as though growth were something that did not concern it; or rather, as if growth served objectives contrary to their interests by means which impinged upon their rights.

It is true that the disparity in earnings is getting worse, that unemployment is spreading, and that the weak are badly protected. It is true that French institutions leave no place, or give no chance, to those at the bottom of the social ladder. Education, the stock market, and real estate—all those institutions are marked by social discrimination and are incapable of meeting the needs of the majority. At a time when experts say that the economy's flexibility and dynamism depend above all on the behaviour of wage earners, most of these wage earners retain the status and the mentality of a minority. This is a lag totally incompatible with a better management of resources.

For a long time American business leaders thought they had found the secret of output in time-clocks and Frederick Taylor's production norms. Since then, however, they have learned that their productivity goals can be reached only through a more intelligent participation by the wage earners. Today we are witnessing an analogous situation on a much larger scale.

Will wage earners accept changes in industry? Will they increase their savings proportionate to the investment needs of our time? Will they allow their salary increases to be adjusted within the framework of an 'in-depth' planning programme? What rights and powers should they be granted, what objectives should be assigned to growth so that they will play their role and show a concern about production? Such are the terms of a dialectic that could stimulate the simultaneous growth of economic efficiency and social justice; such are the elements of a far-reaching 'negotiation' that a Left faithful to its vocation must attempt, and succeed in accomplishing.

The achievement of the Common Market is not the prelude to a new period of stability, but rather the beginning of a period of perpetual change. Automation and computers will become more common, the pace of innovation will speed up, earnings will continue to rise and consumer tastes to vary. Growth will repeatedly sacrifice certain abilities and fields of economic activity, even while creating others.

Suppose that, under the pressure of competition, government and management impose a harsh and 'realistic' conception of industrial conversion, getting rid of all unprofitable enterprises regardless of opposition. This method would have the advantage of simplicity, for it would cut short all discussion. Applied to a society where there is little mobility, it would cause massive strikes and create a class of unemployables. Its effects would be so unbearable that even advocates of modernization through the natural laws of the market would concede that these changes would have somehow to be humanized to prevent events which are normal in a growing economy from being felt like a plague.

This brings us to the heart of the paradox. Labour as a whole has everything to gain from changes that increase productivity and also the number of skilled jobs. The transformation of industrial structures coincides generally with a mass movement toward more interesting and better-paid jobs.

This fact is not lost on wage earners. French workers are far from being consistently hostile to mobility. The sentimental attachment to a job, a business, or a locality is less of an obstacle than the problem of rehousing, work for women, the education of children, the fear of losing professional status, or a leap into the unknown. We have seen from observation that mobility is generally accepted, and even sought, if it is accompanied by certain guarantees.

'After 1950, during years when the productivity demands began seriously to change industrial techniques, qualifications, and the organization of production units, analysts expected to find strong opposition from the workers involved. As it happened, there were such reactions only in cases where the changes put the workers in a *dead-end economic* situation. . . . In the studies we have made, we have noted an *acceptance in principle* of technological change. The protests concerned the human aspects of the changes involved.'[4]

Wage earners have an interest in change. Studies indicate that under certain conditions they will support it. Yet they are afraid, and their unions, in general, fight against it. This nervousness dangerously slows down the modernization of our industrial machine. European governments allowed this attitude to harden for years after the signing of the Treaty of Rome. It was

[4] Guy Barbichon and Serge Moscovici, *Situations de changements et comportements collectifs* (SEDEIS 1967).

not until 1966 that they finally became concerned about professional training, and not until 1967 that they tried to deal with the social problems involved in modernization.

Political leaders have not understood that *in an expanding economy social justice is the condition of industrial dynamism.* Adaptation to technological progress necessarily involves changes in the condition of wage earners, changes which are totally different than the distribution of a few symbolic shares. It demands that the schools provide everyone, not just a favoured minority, with the intellectual tools that will allow them to make one or several changes of job and locale during their active life; that access to culture and the means of professional promotion be vastly increased; that job instability be compensated for by a guaranteed income during periods of reclassification and retraining; that the system of housing loans be reformed so that moving from one part of the country to another becomes easy even for the poor. It is impossible to make the economy more flexible without freeing workers from anguish and fetters of all kinds, both physical and mental, which inhibit their own development and that of industrial production as well.

No doubt within the next few years we will see the need for an industrial strategy. Developments in forecasting will allow us to prepare for the long-range conversion of condemned sectors of the economy, to concentrate our efforts on those that have a future, and to orient labour, both present and future, toward useful jobs instead of hiring workers and then abandoning them in dead-ends. But the more ambitious our efforts to rationalize the movements of labour, the more urgent is our need for concerted action.

Plans which affect a man's occupation, his place of residence, and his way of life—all the principal elements of his existence—will encounter passive resistance or even sabotage if they are conceived and applied without the participation of those involved. To be convinced, workers have to be given specific information on the reasons for the contemplated changes, shown the difficulties involved, brought into decisions about the methods that will be applied, and consulted through their representatives about the necessary contracts. In short, they have to be recognized, and not simply manipulated.

In a free society, either those whose fate is directly involved participate in the work of rationalizing the economy or this work does not take place. We could give up this freedom and move workers around as though they were soldiers; we could give up rationality, let nature take its course, and resign ourselves to waste. But if we want to enjoy the amenities of freedom and the resources of scientific creativity, the way to reconcile them is to increase democracy.

The Western nations have chosen to prevent rapid inflation either by keeping a permanent pool of unemployed, or by emptying and filling it periodically through deflationary policies. In trying to correct the faulty estimates in our drive towards social well-being, we have not made an effort to create a better understanding of the physical possibilities of the economy. Instead we have chosen to cut back our productive capacity. In France the cost of taking such a path has been at least a one-point reduction in the yearly growth rate. Yet one growth point more over a ten-year period could transform the face of the nation.

'Suppose that production grows by 4 per cent a year. If today the level is 100, in ten years it will be 148. Now imagine that we succeed in raising the rate to 5 per cent. The difference seems minimal. Yet over a ten-year period it will bring the level up to 163, or 10 per cent above what we would achieve with a 4-per-cent growth rate. If, instead of dividing this additional wealth among everyone, according to their initial income, suppose that we decided to use all of it to help the more disadvantaged half of the country. The standard of living of this group, which in France number 25 million people, would increase by 90 per cent over a ten-year period, while even those who had not benefited from this addition would see their standard of living rise by 40 per cent during the same period.'[5]

To achieve such an extraordinary goal, we have to regulate, by one means or another, the movement of income, and particularly that of wages, which forms the critical element in industrial societies. The Dutch, the Swedes, and more recently the British have started on this long and arduous path. All have suffered disappointments, including the Swedes, who are the most advanced in this area. They continue to persevere, beginning

[5] Jacques Meraud, *L'Expansion dans la stabilité.*

with Mr. Wilson, whose ideas are slowly budging the trade unions.

In France the arguments of Pierre Massé have met with a political resistance far more than with rational objections. The largest trade union, the CGT, has not rejected the principle, but has declared that 'in a capitalist society the conditions for a national wage policy have not been met.' More imaginative groups have reacted favourably. For the plan to have worked, the government would have had to make a determined attempt to win the confidence of the workers. This, however, was not its principal concern.

These fumbling efforts would cast doubt on the future of a national wage policy if there were any other means of assuring strong and continuing growth. But there aren't. Partisans of national planning can hardly contradict their own argument by saying that everything should be regulated except wages. Those who are suspicious of organized systems, but measure the amount of loss due to stop-and-go expansion, are forced to recognize that the classic tools of political economy are unable to solve the problem. Impelled by a logic common to all Western countries, parallel studies are now going on in Scandinavia, Britain, the Common Market countries, even in the United States.

The fact is that difficulties are due less to the technical complications of such an effort than to its political dimensions. Its application assumes a high degree of coordination from the various players of the economic game, and thus a level of responsibility from labour that it has so far been absent. The foundation of a national wage policy is 'on the Left', in the precise sense of the word, just as yesterday the fundamentals of monetary policy were 'on the Right'.

Technically, the key to a wage policy lies in control of salaries. But no democratic government could propose such controls without at the same time regulating non-salary income through indirect methods. To control this increase in these incomes, it is first necessary to know where they come from, and then to command an effective mechanism for redistributing them. But this mechanism is warped, and the real resources of the privileged classes are swathed in mystery. Will a right-wing government encourage the *strengthening of labour unions*, an essential element of a national wage policy? For a government that believes in economic freedom there can be no question of implementing a wage policy by force. Nor, on the other hand, is it possible to be satisfied with simple recommendations. The principles of freedom and a commitment to economic growth together work in favour of labour. They call for the development of labour unions strong enough to negotiate, make agreements, and keep their promises.

Whether or not the contracts are detailed, whether they include the whole complex of economic activities or only those whose condition could cause imbalances, or whether they come as parallel decisions, does not much matter here. What counts is the existence of an agreement based on mutual consent, and a way of making sure it is respected.

Labour unions that are divided and weak are always hesitant about making commitments. To be in the same league with management and the government in complex negotiations involving far-reaching consequences, they need to have scores of experts at their disposal and millions of members behind them. To impose the necessary discipline on the mass of wage earners, they would have to rely on a great many leaders able to defend the interests of the workers, but also able to understand and to make labour accept the need for a joint strategy. Such a framework demands training methods far superior to anything our unions now have.

To change these weak and disorganized groups into mass organizations equipped with the technical and financial tools of the new industrial era will take years, and will exceed the strength of the labour union movement acting alone. It will demand all the patience, ability, and energy of governments determined to achieve real structural reforms—*reforms that affect the balance of power in society*. It is no longer a question of distributing fictitious rights to workers, but of helping them forge instruments for their participation in the realities of power. It also means re-examining the very objectives of economic expansion.

There is no reason for workers to submit to wage discipline if their standard of living—and, more generally, the condition of their lives—is not improved as a result. Only the appeal of the end result—expressed in concrete terms, such as housing, the future of their children, cultural advantages, shorter work hours, and access to leisure facilities—can persuade them to play by the new economic rules.

If expansion is clearly the base for a new social justice, then *justice becomes the condition of continuing growth*, which is much stronger. This joining of two factors we have habitually seen as separate, or even opposed (what was 'given' from a concern for justice was considered as 'taken' out of production), should be a source of strength for a management-minded Left.

The Left has promised to transform society and has, as long as it has existed, made common cause with the less fortunate. It remains the chosen party of millions of people, nearly half of our citizens, whose lives could be transformed by faster and better-directed growth. To this expectation the Left can make two replies:

1. Exploit the *capital of confidence* it enjoys among wage earners to obtain greater expansion, and then negotiate the advantages thus secured from all social classes to obtain a different distribution of the society's income. In this case it would agree to help make the economy work. It need not lose sight of the conflict of interests, but it would accept their resolution by cooperation and contractual agreements—no longer behaving as though it were involved in a civil war.

2. Exploit the *capital of discontent* that it is equally well placed to take advantage of; wash its hands, by the same token, of the problem of management; and give up the idea of any prolonged exercise of power—these three propositions being closely linked.

It is impossible simultaneously to sow revolt and a sense of responsibility, to train a militia of agitators and an army of efficient managers, to deny economic restraints when in the opposition and recognize them when in power.

Under the second, and more easier, hypothesis, the Left would not be totally reduced to impotence; it could wring concessions from conservatives when they hold the levers of power. And it could profit, as it has done, from the rare and brief moments when it is in power, to pass progressive social legislation. The Right would respect these reforms, and 'digest' them during the following ten years.

But ten years of continuous and organized expansion at the

rate of 5·5 per cent a year would produce results spectacularly superior to those of 40 years of occasional 'assaults'.

Only one motive would justify the resignation of the new political generation to the second method, and that is if the Left were too heavily burdened with men and ideas unable to adapt to the task of supporting a government project. Having no other political base than discontent, the Left would have to satisfy itself, as the young conservative leaders advise it to do, with playing the secondary role of counterweight.

Without doubt this attitude exists among certain men on the Left, who share with their conservative colleagues a deep scepticism about the ability of the common people to assume the full obligations and rewards of citizenship. But there is no objective basis for this.

The desire for progress, it is clear, is steadily winning out over the need to protest. After decades of stagnation, Europeans are converting en masse to the conditions of growth. On the whole, they accept the idea of change more easily than their leaders. The hope which once sustained the revolutionary impetus has not died out in our countries, where so many men still live in mediocrity. This hope now rests on the tangible and honourable gratifications promised by an economy in continual expansion. The Left can, if it chooses, give growth, by its union with justice, the scope of a revolution.

CHAPTER 24

INVESTMENT IN MAN

TEN years ago people did not ask *if* the Russians would reach the American standard of living, but when they would go beyond it. Experts who could hardly be suspected of sympathy for the Soviet regime speculated on the date when the two curves would intersect. 1970? 1985?

In 1968 Soviet agriculture remains petrified in the kolkhoz system and commerce in the state-owned stores. The 'great leap forward' took place in the United States, whose production increases every two years by an amount equal to Britain's total annual output, and whose capacity for innovation astonishes foreign managers and scholars alike.

Obviously Americans are not more intelligent than other people. Yet human factors—the ability to adapt easily, flexibility of organizations, the creative power of teamwork—are the key to their success. Beyond any single explanation, each of which has an element of truth, the secret lies in the confidence of the society in its citizens. This confidence often seems rather naïve to Europeans, but America places it both in the ability of its citizens to decide for themselves, and in the capacity of their intelligence.

A century ago Tocqueville saw this as an essential, indeed the fundamental, characteristic of the New World. 'Each individual, whoever he may be, possesses the degree of intelligence necessary to manage those affairs which concern him exclusively —this is the great principle on which civil and political society rests. The father applies it to his children, the master to his servants, the community to its citizens, the county to its communities, the state to its counties, and the federal union to the states. Taken as a whole, it becomes the dogma of popular

183

sovereignty. . . . From this comes the belief that the individual is the best judge of his own particular interests.'[1]

This optimism which marks every aspect of American life is expressed in the confidence in universal suffrage for direct election of the President. We find the same confidence in the authority delegated to local government to administer everyday aspects of life and to make decisions in the fields of city planning, health, and education—decision-making powers our central government would be terrified to put into the hands of elected officials. We see it again in the catalytic role of research, where ideas are not ornaments, but tools to change the world. And nothing is more *profitable* than a good idea. In the United States adult education is considered an investment, not a form of humanitarianism.

In a small committee of the Productivity Section, French businessmen discuss the advantages of 'periodic recycling' for their executives. But how many of them would dare make a bet on intelligence by gambling engineer-hours—even to win them back again many times over in increased productivity?[2]

By contrast, the French subsidiary of IBM spends 10 per cent of its total payroll on the continual training of its personnel. Visitors from Europe have observed that American universities have been invaded by adults wanting to learn new skills. This same American determination and optimism explain the introduction of scientific methods into areas which until now have been marked by routine.

Contrary to the old cliché, American society gambles much more money on human intelligence than it wastes on gadgets. As we have seen, scientific studies are beginning to confirm what intuition led us to suspect: *this wager on man is the origin of America's new dynamism.* Despite important changes over

---

[1] Alexis de Tocqueville, *Democracy in America.*

[2] Jacques Maisonrouge tells of an incident he witnessed: 'An institute had organized a three-week seminar for executives, and a European firm sent one of its directors to the course. But after a week and a half they called him back because the problems of the business seemed more important and more urgent than the training of a better executive. But since this firm had already paid the admission fee, they decided to send someone else to take the other week and a half of the course!'

the past twenty years, European society, particularly in France, presents a very different picture.

Without doubt France is the country where people are most suspicious of their neighbours. Lawrence Wylie singled out as a serious obstacle to progress 'the French assumption that men are naturally hostile and selfish. . . . Because the French assume that men are hostile, they have protected themselves from "the others" by a complicated network of legality quite in keeping with the French tendency to limit and define carefully all aspects of man's existence. The resultant legal straitjacket quite naturally inhibits change.'[3]

Despite the prestige enjoyed by intellectuals in France, and despite the cult of Cartesian rationality, in reality there exists an evident contempt for ideas, or at least for their practical applications. This is manifested as much in industry by the underdevelopment of research as in government by the security of administrative research services and above all by a lack of interest in them. Best to avoid these 'dead-ends' if you have career ambitions. In both business and government, brain power is badly integrated into the organization.

This scepticism towards man's potential is common to both the Left and the Right, but it results in opposite conclusions. On the Right it leads to the sanctification of the 'natural laws of the market'.

At a time when the nations of Eastern Europe are trying to get back to such economic mechanisms as the price system, interest rates, and profits, it is hard to deny that the market economy is, as Churchill once said about democracy, 'the worst, except for all the others.' It has its obvious limitations. But where competition comes into play, the market provides services that a giant computer programmed by supermen could hardly perform: it points out consumer needs, regulates investment according to demand and cost of materials, and shows by means of deficits which production is unnecessary and which behaviour inefficient. The market provides a place for freedom that the Russians would like to be able to utilize, so that they could get a better return from their economic machine.

However, general decisions affecting the whole economy

[3] From *In Search of France* (Cambridge, Mass.: Harvard University Press, 1963), pp. 207, 208.

result from the statistical sum of millions of individual choices. Taken together, they are not deliberate and free. Rather, they represent an external restraint, a limitation imposed upon everyone by no one in particular. 'The Plan,' said the economist Oscar Lange, 'comes from the need to go beyond the limits of private rationality.' It is an effort to reduce the element of chance and to direct growth towards deliberately chosen objectives. Thus it is an attempt to gain an added margin of liberty.

It is striking that conservatives are more attached to the fetters imposed by the pure market economy on the collective will than to the liberties it provides to individual initiative? Even today they are apt to ask the government simultaneously to release them from the discipline of the Plan and also, by closing professions or frontiers, to spare them the risks of competition.

They are partisans of a society where strongly accentuated 'natural hierarchies' are perpetuated by heredity or by entrenched positions. But the market economy tends to destroy powers that have outlived their economic usefulness. When conservatives invoke the 'natural laws' of the market, they try to give economic mechanisms the untouchable character of something sacred. The charter presented by the French management organization in January 1965—the very year the Fifth Economic Plan was drawn up—extols the 'natural laws of the market' without even mentioning a word about economic planning. Nature itself, the force of circumstances, is involved in the heart of the manifesto to protest against the sacrilege of the Plan and the presumtuousness of human thought and will. 'Of the tree of knowledge of good and evil, thou shalt not eat,' says the Bible. 'For in what day soever thou shalt eat of it, thou shalt die.' The market economy thus serves as a guard rail put up by Providence against the ambitions of men who dangerously believe that they can choose their future.

On the Left the same distrust of man leads to a cult of coercive planning. Many 'progressives' still dream of setting up a society, where an omniscient bureaucracy, the repository of moral order, will dictate to consumers the enlightened decisions they are incapable of making for themselves. To listen to them, it would seem that the mass of people want only to make their hovels more ugly and their cars more beautiful, that the real reason for the housing crisis is not so much the rigidity of rent control and the chaos of the real estate market as an insatiable popular appetite for immediate pleasures, intensified by a docile obedience to advertising. The Left neglects to seek remedies in better information and more effective competition that would lead to increased freedom. It has got into the habit of reinforcing regulations and putting economic activities under rigid control.

When they speak of the excesses of 'the consumer society', many intellectuals of the older generation are really attacking the consumer's right to determine his own needs. The condemnation of this small, but precious, aspect of economic democracy indicates a resurgence of 'enlightened despotism'. An elite convinced of its own wisdom is certain it has the right to impose its own preferences through specific restraints. It would even be ready, so it says, to *restore poverty* in order to protect the masses against the *moral* risks of growth in an atmosphere of freedom.

Let us listen to Simone de Beauvoir: 'In every country of the world, socialist or capitalist, man is crushed by technology, alienated from his work, enslaved and brutalized. This has happened because man has multiplied his needs rather than containing them. Instead of seeking an abundance which does not exist, and may never exist, he should content himself with a vital minimum, as is still the case in certain very poor communities in Sardinia and Greece, for example, where technology has not penetrated and money has not corrupted. There people know an austere happiness because certain values have been preserved; truly human values of dignity, fraternity, and generosity which give life a special flavour. So long as we continue to create new needs, we multiply frustrations. When did this downfall begin? The day that we began to prefer science to wisdom and utility to beauty. With the Renaissance came rationalism, capitalism, and all the isms of science. So be it. But now that we have arrived at this point, what can we do? Try to revive wisdom and a taste for beauty in ourselves and around ourselves. Only a moral revolution, not a social, political, or technological one, can bring man back to his lost truth.'[4]

These two currents of Right and Left, one sanctifying the

[4] Simone de Beauvoir, *Les Belles Images* (Paris: Gallimard, 1966).

market economy from distrust of the audacities of the Plan, the other making a controlled economy an end in itself from fear of the freedoms of the marketplace, combine into a negative 'colbertism',[5] centralist and suspicious of the government. Its behaviour is characterized by lack of a coherent design for the whole, but strictly regulated separation of the activities of each person. It cares a good deal about means and little about ends. Instead of defining objectives precisely, and leaving to those who carry them out the greatest latitude in the choice of methods, it details the methods without deciding upon the long-range objectives.

The head of a government office usually has only a vague idea of the objectives assigned to him, and will promptly define the role of his office by the classic formula, 'exercising responsibility is the framework of rules in operation.' But the means necessary to attain these obscure ends are scrupulously codified in regulations. He does not have the authority to buy an adding machine with funds at his disposal (even if this will save money), nor to send a colleague out of town without permission from the comptroller. The president of a state-owned firm does not always know exactly what the government's policy is in the area where he is supposed to operate; but all the techniques of control and 'guardianship' will guide him step by step so that he avoids all risk.

The choice of 'good management' for maximum growth is not primarily a *technical* choice. It depends, first of all, on the answer to the question: do we or do we not have confidence in the maturity and intelligence of the majority? Until now Europe has answered no. If it decides to say yes, this choice would have unlimited consequences and could change the face of our societies. This act of confidence would be the single source of three policies that form a unity: investing in man's intelligence, liberating his initiative, and seeking a conscious choice of our collective future.

In theory everyone agrees on the first point—the expansion of teaching, professional training, and research. Everyone admits that our lag in national education sterilizes much of our

[5] Jean Baptiste Colbert, French minister of finance in the seventeenth century, followed a policy of protectionism, based on high tariffs, government-controlled trade, and balanced budgets.

intellectual potential, that the inadequacy of professional training is one of the major causes of the rigidity of our industry, and that the poverty of our research threatens to make us an economic satellite.

During the last few years, efforts have been made to correct this three-way deficiency, as is shown by increased appropriations for education. But it is obvious that confidence is in short supply and that a coherent plan does not exist. A 'brain-power policy' is not seen as a necessity that would make its impact felt everywhere it was applied. Outside of teaching and research, where a very great deal still remains to be done, enormous gaps elsewhere reveal the absence of a broad view of the problem, of a well thought-out project, or of a belief in the work to be accomplished.

A project aiming at the full employment of our intellectual resources—and the scarcity of these resources is one of the most dangerous of all 'bottlenecks'—cannot be limited to teaching reform. Other equally important means must be put into action. Adult education is one of them. The effectiveness of the engineer, the professor, the civil servant, and the journalist could be multiplied two or three times if instead of exhausting within a few years the skills he learned at school, he renewed them several times during his active life. A single multiplication would bring great benefits to the society. But think what a second would do!

The second multiplication would consist simply of increasing responsibilities at every level, of placing a bet on trust. In every profession there are men who would produce phenomenally if they were given more initiative, and if, together with greater responsibilities, they had the desire and the occasion to learn, to think, and to act.

Investing in brain power is not enough. We must stop holding it back for fear that it might be put to bad use. Evidence for this is beginning to appear in the crisis in our administrative system, which is characterized by the fear of delegating authority. This fear has shaped whole organizations, justified administrative procedures, and dictated behaviour. Today it has debilitated entire sectors of the economy, where the level of present management is scandalous compared with norms in the most advanced countries.

Public hospitals have never been models of administrative efficiency. But as their equipment becomes more modern, their management becomes even more hopelessly archaic. They buy cobalt equipment for radiotherapy, but their pay scale prevents them from hiring the nurses they need to make practical use of the new machines. They hire the best doctors, but the public agency that runs the hospitals shackles them with regulations of another era.

Ten years ago the P and T (the French Post and Telecommunications system) functioned like a precision clock and enjoyed an enviable reputation. Today, rich in skilled administrators and engineers from the Polytechnique, it is falling apart. In some French cities it takes two years to get a telephone installed, and trunk lines are so overloaded that people have given up making long-distance calls. Yet the French bureaucracy continues to display its unfathomable suspicion of telephone subscribers in a brochure written in pure penitentiary style: 'In case of fraud, offensive behaviour, or insulting speech towards telephone personnel, the company may temporarily suspend use of the instrument. . . . If the subscriber's behaviour is exceptionally serious, the company may at any time, even before the expiration of the minimum subscription period, cancel the service of said subscriber, after having given due notice.'

What has gone wrong? Growing needs and technical progress have speeded up the *rate of change*—but there are still brakes on the initiative that would allow such huge organizations to adapt to change. What the crisis in the hospitals and the telephone service reveals is the failure of a system based on the presumption that government employees and customers are incapable of behaving reasonably. It is enough to read the decrees that appear in the *Journal Officiel* and look at the methods of decision-making to understand that in such a system the principal of a primary school is presumed to be incapable of buying pencils, the president of the government-owned railroads of making an important investment or firing a colleague, a city government of planning its own urban renewal. *The presumption of incompetence spreads in concentric circles.*

A major American corporation has worked out what it calls the 'Ten Basic Principles of Modern Management':

1. Decentralization puts decision-making power as near the arena of action as possible;

2. Decentralization yields the best over-all results if a quick understanding of the problem is applied together with a thorough and relevant knowledge of the facts;

3. Decentralization can work only if there is a real delegation of power, not if it is necessary continually to account for decisions or, even worse, secure prior permission for them;

4. Decentralization implies confidence that people who carry out such decentralized responsibilities will be able to make the right decisions in most cases; this confidence must come from the head office;

5. Decentralization demands a realization that the basic role of headquarters consists in providing aid and advice, through a relatively small number of qualified people, so that administrators can make decisions with a full knowledge of all the relevant factors;

6. Decentralization requires a recognition that the combination of several individually good decisions is worth more to the firm and to everyone than decisions made and controlled by a central office;

7. Decentralization rests on the need to give the firm general objectives, organized methods of communication, policies and control devices which are known, understood, and followed; but it must be kept in mind that the choice of a policy does not necessarily imply uniformity in the methods for carrying it out;

8. Decentralization can take place only if the directors understand that they cannot themselves retain the authority they delegated to their colleagues at lower levels;

9. Decentralization can be effective only if responsibility proportional to the decision-making power of each individual is accepted and supported at all levels;

10. Decentralization requires a personnel policy based on evaluation of performance, respect for objectives, promotions based on achievement, and dismissal for incapacity or inadequate results.[6]

[6] Cited by Olivier Giscard d'Estaing, founder of the management school at Fontainebleau, in his book, *La décentralisation des pouvoirs dans l'entreprise.*

Turning these principles upside down would give a reasonably exact picture of the hierarchy of relations in Europe: distrust of superiors towards subordinates suspected of incompetence, of subordinates towards superiors suspected of despotism, of most people towards immediate, and thus personalized, authority. This leads to such consequences as decision-makers who are far removed from the arena of action, proliferation of impersonal rules dictating the smallest details of behaviour, stratification of the hierarchy which prevents a normal circulation of information, multiplication of preventive controls, general promotion by seniority, etc. At every level *distrust* has become an institution.

The presumption of incompetence causes a double distortion. It kills initiative within the person and within the organization, and it throws the administrative structure out of joint. A central office so bogged down in details and the coordination of millions of individual operations can have only a fictitious unity.

The presumption of incompetence produces its own confirmation, for it does not allow those it strikes the opportunity to demonstrate or acquire the expertise which they are refused a priori. It breeds irresponsible conduct, thus justifying the suspicion on which it is based. Neither Sweden nor the United States nor Switzerland, each of which implements a far greater degree of decentralization, experiences such aberrations.

Even if its task were lightened, the government would not be short of work to do. It could concentrate on those responsibilities no one else can assume. Administrators and civil servants could devote their efforts to the essential element of their profession—defining objectives carefully, and working out policies with precision. Large modern corporations tend to 'centralize objectives and decentralize decisions.' As a huge enterprise, the government ought to follow the same rule. The source of its inefficiency is not so much the lack of financial or juridical means, as the absence of clear objectives and coherent policies.

It is not only the government, but all of European society that is adrift. But isn't it precisely the role of those who exercise power, or pretend to, to save us from indecision? They will never succeed unless they decide to 'have done' a great deal of what they now do themselves and which is more than they can handle. Centralization spares those in command the need to explain their objectives to others, or even to themselves, while decentralization forces them to do so.

It is not possible to show initiative without running the risk of error, any more than there can be responsibility without sanctions. Every attempt to free initiative implies a control over the results. The market, where it really works, is one of these methods. Renault considers its methods of management 'controlled' by the competition of Citroën or Volkswagen a thousand times more strongly and rigorously than by the 'guardianship' of the government ministry responsible for it. The establishment, or re-establishment, of effective competition would invigorate closed or restricted professions much better than refining government regulations. Competition is written into the definition of the Common Market, and there is no reason to be sorry that this risks doing away with tight controls.

There are other sanctions that can be used when those of the market do not apply. The decisions of the electorate at the polls could well replace the guardianship of the central government over questions of municipal government. If mayors and municipal councillors would become truly responsible for the management of their communities, and if the communities would finance the services for which they are responsible out of their own resources, the voters would clearly see the link between the fiscal effort demanded of them and the results achieved by the municipality. They could then judge good or bad management by their votes. However imperfect democratic control may be, it is infinitely preferable, simply from the viewpoint of efficiency, to a system which eliminates all control by making it impossible to know who is responsible.

Where neither the market nor the ballot box made it possible to reconcile responsibility with freedom of action, all that remain are modern rules of management. *What counts is the determination to liberate initiative and show confidence in man at every level.* All who are capable of learning and acting, but cannot do so because they are not given responsibility, would bring the community an invaluable supply of skills.

Although no government has yet sought such an objective, it involves a *political project* of the greatest urgency, for everything else depends on it, and will be affected by it. Some urge us

to wait until the natural evolution of customs and gradual disintegration of the old system bring this project into being. But
history offers too many examples of civilizations slowly drowned
by the weight of their own past.

The liberation of initiative is not one of those problems that
party platforms like to deal with. But it is an absolutely crucial
political operation. It cannot be undertaken without being
desired, and it cannot be desired unless political officials themselves shed the scepticism that permeates our society. This same
guideline can help them in making choices with a greater consciousness of the directions the economy is taking.

The acceleration of the growth rate and advances in forecasting call for more precise long-range goals. The rising standard of living dramatizes the lag in public facilities—on which
the quality of our lives depends increasingly—as compared to
individual consumption. While the market is a useful indicator
of a large range of needs, it is not able to point out those which
should be first on our list of priorities if we want to build a more
livable society. Operations as crucial as the expansion of electronics research or the civilian use of atomic breeders are so
far-reaching that private firms must work together, under
government leadership and with the help of public funds. This
is not the moment to suggest the disengagement of the government, but rather to propose that it concentrate its resources on
the supreme responsibilities no one else can assume in its place.

We can ask for both more planning and more freedom without getting involved in a political battle of words. 'The dialectic
between the Plan and the market has become much more
refined,' says François Bloch-Lainé. 'By combining American
developments in management with French experiments in
flexible, coherent planning, we can be revolutionary simply by
being more aware of what we are doing.'

Despite traditional ways of thinking on both the Right and
the Left, liberation of initiative and control over acts which
open the gates to the future are two parts of a single emancipa-
tion. It goes without saying that there is no end of difficult
reconciliations to make between the freedom of individuals and
the strategy of the government. But experience denies that there
is a fundamental antagonism between the two.

The logic of liberalism and the logic of detailed government planning are equally wobbly because both amputate a part of man's creative power. Confidence and liberty are linked by the common inspiration that Jaurès evoked when he outlined his idea of the objectives of Marxism:

'Marx said that until now human society has been governed by fatality and the blind movement of economic forces; that institutions and ideas are not the conscious work of free men, but the reflection in the human brain of man's life in society. We are still in the stage of pre-history. Human history will truly begin only when man, escaping from the tyranny of unconscious forces, will be able to control production itself by his reason and his will.'[7]

Nearly the same expressions have come from the pen of a modern technocrat like Pierre Massé: 'The impetus for this great work of social and economic development is the freedom and the will of man. Its instruments are plans, general or specific, private or public, which in their most diverse forms have consciousness and intent as their common denominator, rather than fatality and chance.'

If the theory of planning has made great strides since 1945, its practice has been a good deal slower. This is not because the government—which controls the budget, taxes, the nationalized banks, and is private industry's biggest client—is short of power, for if anything, it has an excess. Rather it is because it hesitates, from a scepticism about this 'calculated risk', to be more consistent in its own efforts. Most experts believe that rationalizing the government bureaucracy would yield spectacular advances in planning.

To gain more freedom we will have to go down into the storeroom of public funds and probably change our machinery completely. The Americans started this in July 1967 by vigorously applying the PPBS—Planning, Programming, Budgeting System. Under the grim exterior of a new budgeting system, the PPBS has become the point of departure for a revolution in the technique of government. It is a revolution inspired by all the optimism of the scientific spirit. The stake is nothing less than the abolition of routine and precedent, those ancient, legendary, and universal causes of bureaucratic delay. To do

---

[7] Jean Jaurès, *Introduction à l'histoire socialiste.*

this they will introduce output factors, cost-efficiency programmes, and even project competition into all decision-making
areas.

The object of the system, of course, is not to spare the
government or the Congress political options. No list of figures
can tell us whether it is better to launch a programme for better
education or for space research. The important choices are
based on a conviction of what is important. Reformers have
tried to clarify choices and force officials from one end of the
hierarchy to another to think seriously about their course of
action and to engage in it with a full knowledge of their objectives. The new system of budgeting is basically a kind of instruc-
tion, an attempt to help intelligence triumph over routine.

Who will be more capable of this act of confidence on which
good management depends—the Right or the Left? 'Nature,'
says Ramuz, 'tends to the right.' The Right has never stopped
opposing nature to artifice, that is, to human inventions. Not
that the Right doesn't know how to make use of artifices from
time to time. But it disguises them as 'natural laws' in order to
pose obstacles to conscious choice. We have recently seen the
resurrection of financial taboos which were seemingly killed
long ago by experience and the laws of economics: the taboo of
the gold standard, imposed on nations because of the natural
and intrinsic qualities of the metal; the taboo of the balanced
budget, which, if it were ever really applied, would deprive the
government of the budget deficit necessary, in certain cases, to
counteract recessions.

There is no natural wine, said Jaurès. 'Bread and wine are a
product of man's genius. Even nature itself is a wonderful
human artifice.' This is an affirmation that the Right has always
contested. René Rémond, the best historian of the Right, dis-
tinguishes three reasons for doing so which he says combine in
an 'innate scepticism for everything that seeks to deviate from
the natural course of things, submission to the natural order,
which condemns revolution and the very principle of structural
reform.'[8]

The Right is still, as Lyautey said, 'the government of the
elite,' opposed to an ambitious democracy that urges every man

[8] René Rémond, *Histoire de la droite en France* (1967).

to assume the fullest measure of responsibility of which he is capable. The elite holds on to its rights, and, if necessary, its privileges, from its belief in the innate ineptitude and irremediable inequality of man. The hostility of conservatives to every attempt to change the 'natural order' by a man-made order is motivated by this deep distrust as much as by the desire to defend its material interests.

The recent official animosity in France to a supra-national Europe comes from the same distaste for necessarily arbitrary man-made constructions. 'There is,' said the right-wing thinker Maurras, 'a unity, a political, civic, and social entity called France. There is no Europe, in which to invest, by opposition and symmetry of oratory, similar or corresponding attributes. To speak of France and Europe in terms of concrete politics is about as serious as balancing the antithesis of I and non-I. We know the I; he is a defined person whose name corresponds to a distinct reality. The non-I is anything we might want to include under this floating epithet. It is an abuse of language to put into two equally precise words two ideas so devoid of logical and practical equivalence.'

There was, and still is, a good dose of realism in the scepticism of the Right. It is true that nations are powerful realities, and that the 'light' of reason is unequally distributed. But realism changes sides as men learn to understand the forces that surround them and thereby gain the power to channel and dominate them. The desire to do better, which once inspired utopias, has now become the condition of progress, and even of wisdom. It is this confidence in the possibilities of man that is the soul of the Left.

This is expressed sometimes clumsily, sometimes with vision, but always with a bias for science against obscurantism, for democracy against authoritarianism, for change against the status quo. It has inspired doctrines, and also struggles, which have profoundly marked the history of our country.

The professional conservatism that has taken over the academic world should not make us forget that it is men of the Left, Republican teachers, who led, against an elite eager to retain its monopoly, the battle for the diffusion of knowledge when the going was most difficult. The resistance of the parliamentary circle to the election of the chief of state by direct popular ballot should not let us forget that historically the progress of universal suffrage is due to the tenacity of the Left. It is the Left that brought rational decision-making to the economy, and thanks to the Left that the idea of the Plan came to France.

If we look beyond the methods laid down by the 'founding fathers' to the objectives they sought and the hopes that inspired them, what we find is precisely in the words of Jaurès, 'the eruption of the great, burning, free voice of humanity which, freed from all servitude, will take over the world through science, action, and dream. The day that there will be free passage, free and continuous movement of all forms and functions of human activity, the *changing or unformed aptitudes of men will not be frozen* and immobilized from the beginning by the first professions they go into; *their activities will be continuously revitalized*, and even the slowly-rising sap will be able to open new channels and burst into an unexpected flowering.'

If criticism of an oppressive capitalism led these 'founding fathers' of socialism to challenge the explicit liberties capitalism dispensed to a few thousand of the privileged, it is equally true that they wanted, on the whole, a society of individual initiative. These objectives are completely contemporary. Their vision of an open society where men are *mobile* and continually *regenerated* by continuing education is magnificently confirmed today.

Never have these values been so precious as they are now, when we have glimpsed the vastness of man's resources, and consequently, the historic failure that could come from not developing them.

CONCLUSION

FOR societies, as for men, there can be no growth without challenge. Progress is a battle, just as life is a struggle. We have never been able to forget these truths, because so far human history has been nearly indistinguishable from military history.

Today the industrially advanced societies—the United States, the Soviet Union, Europe—are bringing that era of history to a close. Military confrontations between these great powers can be only hypothetical or thermonuclear. We cannot, of course, exclude the possibility of annihilation. But our point of departure for thought and action must be a hypothesis of atomic peace. The war we face will be an industrial one.

The conflict in Vietnam, that absurd and barbarous residue of the Crusades, will inevitably come to an end. The great majority of Americans are eagerly supporting efforts to reach a negotiated peace so that they may bring to an end an expedition whose sole rational objective was long ago achieved: halting the spread of Chinese imperialism in Asia, as Stalinist imperialism was contained in Europe.

Now we are beginning to discover what was concealed by twenty years of colonial wars, wars that dominated our thoughts and our behaviour: the confrontation of civilizations will now take place in the battlefield of technology, science, and management.

The American expeditionary corps will leave Vietnam, where there is nothing more to gain and everything to lose. But American industry will not leave Europe, where it has made new conquests and increased its formidable power. Even if we were not faced with such a challenge by the Americans, we

199

ought to find in ourselves the power and the desire to build a more intelligent and bountiful post-industrial society. Technological duels and organizational prowess appeal to us, but are less enthralling than the vision of a higher form of civilization. The American challenge really only adds an external pressure to what is an internal necessity.

This unprecedented challenge has found us alone and unprepared, but not without resources. When power was measured by the number of men in arms and the number of legions, Europe was a leader. When power became industrial and was applied to the transformation of raw materials, Europe was still in the front ranks. In 1940 nothing would have been able to defeat a coalition of Germany, Britain, and France, if they were really united. Even when plunged into the most terrible civil war of her history by Hitler's folly, this Europe, her body bled and her spirit drained, revived to make an extraordinary recovery after 1950, and can still aspire to a role of leadership. What our leaders have lacked in this postwar period is a rational ambition—an ambition that can be achieved.

During the years when American industry began its conquest of advanced technology, our political leaders were blind to new realities and the potential of the future. So blind that Britain and France were no better off than defeated Germany and Italy when confronted with the real winner who knew how to exploit his success and is now preparing his greatest triumph.

This new conquest is the perfect definition of 'intangible'. This no doubt explains why it has been misunderstood by leaders accustomed to think in terms of tons of steel, machinery, and capital. The signs and instruments of power are no longer armed legions or raw materials or capital. Even factories are only an external symbol. Modern power is based on the capacity for innovation, which is research, and the capacity to transform inventions into finished products, which is technology. The wealth we seek does not lie in the earth or in numbers of men or in machines, but in the human spirit. And particularly in the ability of men to think and to create.

The scientist accepts this, but the politician, the civil servant, and the businessman understand it only with difficulty. It is fashionable today to praise profit indiscriminately. But as the French economist François Perroux has shown, it is a catch-all for everything: returns on a business, monopoly gains, killings on a speculation. Healthy profit, real profit, for a business as for society as a whole, lies in the *fruits of innovation*.

The training, development, and exploitation of human intelligence—these are the real resources, and there are no others. The American challenge is not ruthless, like so many Europe has known in her history, but it may be more dramatic, for it embraces everything.

Its weapons are the use and systematic perfection of all the instruments of reason. Not simply in the field of science, where it is the only tool, but also in organization and management, where Europeans are used to the irrational—the fetishism of precepts passed down from father to son, the weight of routine, the divine right of authority, and the unjustified priority of flair over systematic thought. In contrast with these entrenched forces, human reason is flexible, light, and mobile.

We can no longer sit back and wait for the renaissance. And it is not going to be evoked by patriotic rhetoric or clarion calls left over from the age of military battles. It can come only from subtle analysis, rigorous thought, and precise reasoning. It calls for a special breed of politicians, businessmen, and labour leaders.

How much time do we have to find them? It would be foolish to set a date. But we know, since each area can be measured, that there is a point of no return, and that it is not far away. There are only a few years left, and if we take electronics as a gauge, very few.

In some areas it is already too late, such as full-scale space exploration and supersonic aviation. But these are not the really vital sectors. The new frontiers of human creativity in every area lie in information systems and their utilization, and the Americans themselves do not seem to fully realize this yet. We must forge ahead into this area before it is taken over by others.

This would be an enormous undertaking. It means utilizing the intelligence of all the qualified men our society can train and equip. Above all, it means they must fight to the full limit of their ability or their skills, and *for their own sake*. This is the political problems par excellence.

In a free society like our own, there is no single political path to follow. Each man should express his ideas, as we have given ours. The debate that follows will shed light and build the strength to follow through. The only condition is that everyone recognize and accept the subject of the debate. This time it is fairly simple. It is not for us to choose, for it is imposed upon us —it is the American challenge. We have only to understand it, to close in upon it, to study it.

This book has no other ambition than to contribute to that task. It is true that it offers no conclusion, for if tragedy is upon us, the final act has not yet been written. In any case, this is not a history book, but, with a little luck, a call to action.

Index

Advanced industrial societies, 25
Africa, investment in, 9
Agfa-Gevaert Company, 5
Air France, 107
Algeria, French investment in, 29
Algerian War, ix, xii
America, *see* Canada; Latin America; United States of America
America in the Common Market (Hellmann), 8, 9
American colossus, the, 37–50
American Express Company, 4
American Telephone and Telegraph Corporation, 62
Americanization, 27–28, 136
Annexation, path of, 139
Aral, 15
Argentina, consumer society, 25
Armand, Louis, 78, 146, 147
Aron, Raymond, 76
Assault on Europe, American, 3–33
Atlantic Pact, 58
Atlanticism, path of, 114–15
Atomic energy, 121
Atomic Energy Commission, 71
Atomic peace, 199
Australia, advanced industrial society, 25
Austria, 126
Automation, 63, 65, 165, 175

Beauvoir, Simone de, 187
Belgium, investment in, American, 12, 133
Bell, Daniel, 24, 24 n.
Bell X5 supersonic plane, 87
Benelux countries, American Investment in, 14
Bertin, Gilles, 9, 10 n.
'Black Arrow' (satellite launcher), 97
Bloch-Lainé, François, 158, 194
'Blue Streak' missile, 92, 93, 95
Blum, Léon, 157, 172
Boeing SST, 84–85, 89, 101
Bolsheviks, 153

Booze, Allen and Hamilton, 6
Boyer de la Giroday, 12, 13
Britain, *see* Great Britain
British Marketing Council, 3
Bruclain, Walter, 8 n.
Budgeting system, 195
Bureau of Mines, U.S., 88
Business cycles, 51

Cambien, Mr., 118
Canada, post-industrial society, 25
Capital investment, factor in economic expansion, 52
Celanese Corporation of America, 4
Census Bureau, U.S., 51, 53, 54
Chamberlain, Neville, 132
Change, corollary of growth, 170–1
mechanics of, 149
Chase Manhattan Bank, 18 n.
Chile, consumer society, 25
China, 144
Chorafas, Dimitri, 54
Chosen generation, the, 139–51
Chrysler Corporation, 14
Churchill, Sir Winston, 132, 185
Coal and Steel Community, 76, 78–79
Cognard, Pierre, 46 n, 47
Colbert, Jean Baptiste, 188 n.
Colbertism, 188
Colombia, consumer society, 25
Commerce Department, U.S., 9, 71, 88
Common Market, *see* European Economic Community
Common Market Commission, 77, 78, 129
Common Sense (Paine), ix
Communal polycentrism, 79
Communards of 1871, 159
Communications, 63, 65, 66
by satellites, 70, 91
new techniques of, 67
Communist Party, French, 159, 163, 164
Italian, 162

203